asian flavors

asian flavors

FABULOUS FOOD of THE FAR EAST

Kim Chung Lee

southwater

This edition is published by Southwater

Southwater is an imprint of Anness Publishing Ltd
Hermes House, 88–89 Blackfriars Road, London SE1 8HA; tel. 020 7401 2077; fax 020 7633 9499; info@anness.com

© Anness Publishing Ltd 2000, 2002

Published in the USA by Southwater, Anness Publishing Inc.
27 West 20th Street, New York, NY 10011; fax 212 807 6813

This edition distributed in the UK by The Manning Partnership
251–253 London Road East, Batheaston, Bath BA1 7RL
tel. 01225 852 727; fax 01225 852 852; sales@manning-partnership.co.uk

This edition distributed in the USA by National Book Network
4720 Boston Way, Lanham, MD 20706; tel. 301 459 3366; fax 301 459 1705; www.nbnbooks.com

This edition distributed in Canada by General Publishing
895 Don Mills Road, 400–402 Park Centre, Toronto, Ontario M3C 1W3; tel. 416 445 3333; fax 416 445 5991; www.genpub.com

This edition distributed in Australia by Sandstone Publishing
Unit 1, 360 Norton Street, Leichhardt, New South Wales 2040; tel. 02 9560 7888; fax 02 9560 7488; sales@sandstonepublishing.com.au

This edition distributed in New Zealand by The Five Mile Press (NZ) Ltd
PO Box 33-1071 Takapuna, Unit 11/101-111 Diana Drive, Glenfield, Auckland 10; tel. (09) 444 4144; fax (09) 444 4518; fivemilenz@clear.net.nz

A CIP catalogue record for this book is available from the British Library.

Publisher Joanna Lorenz
Project Editor Debra Mayhew
Designed by Wilson Harvey; *Food illustrations* Madeleine David, Anna Koska
Recipes by Alex Barker, Kit Chan, Kim Chung Lee, Roz Denny, Rafi Fernandez, Christine France, Sarah Gates,
Shirley Gill, Shehzad Husain, Sallie Morris, Liz Trigg, Deh-Ta Tsuing, Steven Wheeler.
Food photography Karl Adamson, Edward Allwright, David Armstrong, Steve Baxter, James Duncan, Michelle Garrett, Amanda Heywood, Michael Michaels, Juliet Piddington.
Food for photography Kit Chan, Carole Handslip, Shezad Husain, Wendy Lee, Jane Stevenson, Carol Tennant, Steven Wheeler, Elizabeth Wolf-Cohen.
Stylists Madelaine Brehaut, Michelle Garrett, Maria Kelly, Blake Minton, Marion Price, Kirsty Rawlings.

Previously published as *The Magic of Asia*

1 3 5 7 9 10 8 6 4

NOTES

Standard spoon and cup measures are level.

Large eggs are used unless otherwise stated.

CONTENTS

Introduction 6

Appetizers 16

Seafood Dishes 50

Poultry Dishes 82

Meat Dishes 114

Vegetable Dishes 148

Rice and Noodles 180

Desserts 210

Accompaniments 242

Index 252

INTRODUCTION

As the world's largest continent and home to some of the greatest ancient civilizations, it is not surprising that Asia has also developed a noble cuisine to match. Geography, climate, culture and religion have all played their parts in shaping the unique cuisine of Pakistan, India, Thailand, Vietnam, Malaysia, Indonesia, China and Japan. Traders, colonists and tourists later helped to cross-fertilize the techniques and ingredients of these countries, blurring their origins and allowing each nation to put their own culinary stamp on them.

While Asian cuisine reflects these differences, it also shares many common features. Throughout Asia, cooking is a source of personal pride and eating is a pleasurable, social occasion. Asian cooks strive for a harmonious balance of flavours, textures, colours and aromas. Using only the freshest and best-quality ingredients, they prepare them with care to ensure that each flavour is brought out in the dish. A meal includes many dishes, which are all placed on the table at one time and eaten in no particular order. There will always be rice or noodle dishes, a soup, a curry, a steamed or fried dish, a salad and a dipping sauce or relishes.

This book offers an introduction to this diverse and delicious cuisine. Clear, step-by-step instructions make it simple to prepare these dishes at home. In no time you will create curries, make sushi, cook perfect basmati rice, prepare miso soup and assemble spring rolls. With a glossary of all the unusual ingredients and methods, cooks who are new to Asian cooking will find these recipes easy to follow and guaranteed to produce successful dishes. "Priti bhoja', as they say in India, "ching ching", as they say in China, or closer to home, just "enjoy"!

LEFT: (clockwise from top left) fenugreek, curry leaves, and coriander leaves.

GUIDE TO INGREDIENTS

Aduki beans
Small, red beans that are related to the soya bean, used in rice dishes or sweetened and used in desserts; also available in glacé form (ama-natto) or in a paste (neri-an).

Special ingredients give Asian dishes their distinctive tastes: (CLOCKWISE FROM TOP LEFT) Nari, which is also known as pickled ginger; the Chinese spice, star anise; sesame seeds, which can also be toasted.

Almonds
Blanched almonds are available whole, flaked and ground, and impart a sumptuous richness to curries. They are considered a great delicacy in India, where they are extremely expensive.

Aubergines
A vegetable fruit with a mildly sweet flavour. Many varieties of aubergine are used in Thai cooking, from the tiny pea aubergines, which are added just before the end of cooking, to white, green or yellow aubergines. When these types are unavailable, use the purple variety.

Bamboo shoots
The edible young shoots of the bamboo plant. Pale to bright yellow when bought fresh. Fresh bamboo shoots need some preparation and take quite a long time to cook. When buying canned shoots, look out for the whole ones as they seem to be better quality than the ready-sliced canned bamboo shoots.

Banana leaves
Glossy, dark green leaves of the banana tree are used to line steamers or wrap foods such as chicken or fish prior to grilling or baking. They have a slight flavour of fine tea.

Basil
A pungent herb that is used widely in Mediterranean and South-east Asian cooking. Three varieties are used in Thai cooking: *bai mangluk* (hairy basil), *bai horapa* (sweet basil) and *bai grapao* (holy basil). Of these, *bai horapa* is the most popular. It has small, dark leaves with reddish-purple stems and flowers. Its flavour is reminiscent of aniseed and somewhat stronger than that of the western sweet basil.

Basmati rice
Light and fragrant rice grown in the foothills of the Himalayan mountains. Basmati makes the perfect base for pilaff dishes.

Bay leaves
The large dried leaves of the bay laurel tree are one of the oldest herbs used in cookery.

Bean curd
Known also as tofu or dofu, this is a flavourless curd made from soya beans that is rich in vitamins and minerals. It is available fresh, long-life or dried. It is a common ingredient in Chinese dishes and is a good source of protein for vegetarians.

Pungent ingredients add aromatic interest to Asian dishes: (CLOCKWISE FROM TOP LEFT) red and green chillies; bay leaves; garlic.

Bean sauce
Made from salted and fermented soya beans, this sauce is a popular flavouring agent in Oriental dishes. It is also called yellow bean sauce.

Beansprouts
Sprouted from mung beans, they are used in salads and in stir-fried dishes, either raw or cooked. Look for crisp, firm sprouts with little scent.

Bok choy
A Chinese cabbage that has thick white stalks and dark green leaves.

Bonito
The Pacific bonito is a small tuna that is commonly used in Japanese cooking. It is the strongest flavoured of the tuna and is used dried in thin flakes known as katsuo-bushi. The flakes are used to flavour stock and sprinkled over dishes to season.

Cardamom pods
A spice native to India, where its value is considered second only to that of saffron.

Cashew nuts
These full-flavoured nuts are a popular ingredient in many Asian cuisines.

Chana dhal
A round split yellow lentil, similar in appearance to the smaller moong dhal and the larger yellow split pea, which can be used as a substitute. It is used as a binding agent in some dishes and is widely available from Asian stores.

Chapati flour
A type of wholemeal flour used to make chapatis and other breads.

Chick-peas
A nutty tasting pulse that is widely used in Indian vegetarian dishes.

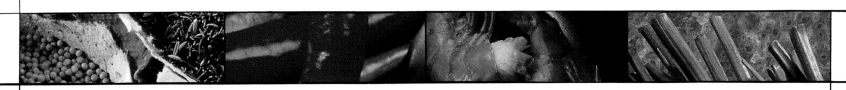

Chillies

Hot peppers in many varieties. Their fire comes from the seeds, which can be removed for a milder flavour. Dried chilli peppers can be used whole or coarsely crushed.

Chilli powder

Also known as cayenne pepper, this is a fiery ground spice which should be used with caution.

(LEFT): Mooli is a long white radish with a peppery flavour. (RIGHT): Tiny pea aubergines add flavour to Thai dishes.

Cinnamon

One of the earliest known spices with an aromatic and sweet flavour. It is sold ready-ground or as sticks.

Cloves

The dried flower bud of a tropical tree, used whole or ground as a spice.

Coconut

Used to flavour both sweet and savoury dishes and can be substituted with desiccated or creamed coconut if necessary.

Coconut milk

The unsweetened liquid made from grated coconut flesh and water, which is an essential ingredient of many Thai dishes. It comes in cans, compressed blocks or in powdered form.

Coriander

Also known as cilantro or Chinese parsley. This is a beautifully fragrant herb from which the leaves, seeds and roots are used in Chinese, Indian and Thai cuisine. It is also used sprinkled over dishes as an attractive garnish.

Coriander Seeds

An aromatic spice with a pungent and slightly lemony flavour. The seeds are used either coarsely ground or in powdered form, in meat, poultry and fish dishes. Ground coriander is an important part of any curry powder.

Cumin

White cumin seeds are oval, ridged and greenish-brown in colour. They have a strong aroma and flavour and can be used whole or ground. Ready-ground cumin powder is widely available. Black cumin seeds are dark and aromatic and are used to flavour curries and rice.

Curry leaves

Similar in appearance to bay leaves but with a very different flavour, they are available dried, and sometimes fresh, from Asian stores. Fresh leaves freeze well.

Curry paste

Traditionally made by pounding fresh herbs and spices together in a mortar. This is a time-consuming process but the finished product tastes delicious and keeps well. Ready-made pastes are good, convenient alternatives.

Dashi

A stock used in Japanese cookery and usually made from kombu seaweed.

Dried mushrooms

These include a variety of mushrooms: black mushrooms, cloud ears and wood ears, which turn meaty and succulent when soaked in water.

Asian dishes feature a large variety of noodles: (FROM LEFT TO RIGHT) cellophane noodles; Somen noodles; egg noodles.

Egg noodles

Made from wheat flour, egg and water. The dough is flattened and shredded to the required shape and thickness.

Enoki mushrooms

Long stems and tiny white caps. They are crisp with a delicate flavour.

Fennel seeds

Very similar in appearance to cumin seeds, with a very sweet taste. These are used to flavour certain curries or can also be chewed as a mouth-freshener after a spicy meal.

Fenugreek

This is available fresh or as seeds. The fresh variety is sold in bunches and has very small leaves which are used to flavour meat and vegetarian dishes. The stalks must be discarded or they will make the food bitter. The seeds are very pungent and slightly bitter.

Fish sauce

The most commonly used flavouring in Thai food, along the lines of soy sauce for Chinese food. It is made from salted anchovies and has a strong salty flavour.

Five-spice powder

A mixture of aniseed, cinnamon, fennel seed, cloves and Szechuan pepper used in Chinese cooking.

Galangal

A member of the ginger family that looks similar to fresh root ginger, but with a more translucent skin and a pinkish tinge. It has a wonderful sharp, lemony taste and is prepared in a similar way to root ginger. Best used fresh, it is also available dried or in powder form.

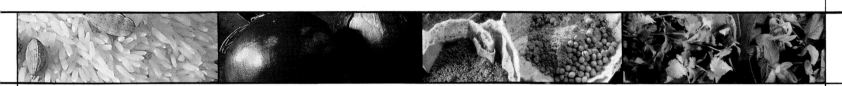

Garam masala

A mixture of Indian spices that can be made from freshly ground spices at home or bought ready-made. A typical mixture might include black cumin seeds, peppercorns, cloves, cinnamon and black cardamom pods.

(LEFT) Onion seeds are widely used in pickles. (RIGHT) Cloves can be used whole to impart flavour, and then removed, or ground as a spice.

Garlic

A very important ingredient in Asian cooking. Look out for fresh shiny heads. Avoid soft, dusty or mouldy cloves. Jars of pickled garlic can be bought from Oriental stores.

Ginger

A root of Chinese and Indian origin. It should either be peeled and chopped or crushed before cooking. Not as popular as galangal in Thai cooking, but a useful alternative. Dried ginger makes a good standby if fresh is not available.

Gobo

A long, thin root vegetable which is also known as burdock. It may be soaked to remove any bitterness and eaten raw or cooked.

Hijiki

Dried seaweed that is soaked and used in soups and salads.

Hoisin sauce

Also known as barbecue sauce, it is made from soya beans and has a dark reddish-brown colour with a hot and sweet flavour.

Kaffir lime

Similar to the common lime but with a knobbly skin. The zest is often used and the dark, glossy, green leaves from the tree give a pungent lemony-lime flavour to soups, curries and other dishes. Bought fresh from Oriental stores, the leaves keep well and can also be frozen. Dried Kaffir limes are also available.

Katakuri–ko

Potato starch or flour; cornflour can be used as an alternative. Available in Oriental shops.

Kelp

Kelp seaweed is used to flavour stock and is also served as a vegetable

Kombu

Dried kombu is a dark grey-brown colour with a pale powdery covering.

Konnyaku

A cake made from flour produced from a root vegetable called devil's tongue. Tear it into pieces before cooking so that it absorbs more flavour. Black and white varieties are both available.

Lemon grass

An aromatic tropical grass which is also known as citronella. Lemon grass characterizes Thai and Vietnamese cuisine. It has a long, pale green stalk and a bulbous end – similar to a spring onion. Only the bottom portion is used and it should be crushed lightly before chopping to release more flavour.

(LEFT) Indian cooking uses bright yellow turmeric to add colour to dishes. (RIGHT) Dried red chillies are extremely hot and can be used whole or crushed.

Lengkuas

A member of the ginger family, available either in fresh, dried or powdered form.

Masoor dhal

Red split lentils which turn pale yellow when cooked.

Mirin

A sweet version of cooking sake, this has a delicate flavour and is usually added in the final stages of cooking.

Miso

A fermented paste of soya beans, which forms the key ingredient of miso soup and is widely used as a seasoning. There are various types of miso, which may be based on barley, wheat or soya bean starter mould. The lightest flavour is from white miso; red miso is saltier while dark brown miso has a stronger flavour.

Mooli

A long white radish which is also called daikon. About the size of a parsnip, mooli has a crunchy texture and peppery flavour similar to red radishes but milder. It may be cooked or served raw in salads.

Moong dhal

Teardrop-shaped split yellow lentils that are similar to, though smaller than, chana dhal.

Mustard seeds

Round in shape and sharp in flavour, black mustard seeds are used for flavouring curries and pickles.

Nari
Pale pink ginger pickles that are served with sushi or sashimi, to refresh the palate between bites.

Noodles
An important ingredient in Chinese, Japanese, Thai and other Asian dishes. Cellophane noodles are made from ground mung beans and are commonly called bean thread, glass or transparent noodles. Dried noodles must be soaked in hot water before using. Egg noodles are made from wheat flour, egg and water. Rice noodles are made from ground rice and water and range in thickness from very thin to wide ribbons and sheets. Rinse rice noodles in warm water and drain well before use. Rice vermicelli is a thin, brittle noodle that looks like white hair and is sold in large bundles. They cook almost instantly in hot liquid, provided the noodles are first soaked in warm water. Soba noodles are made from a mixture of buckwheat and wheat flour. They are traditionally cooked in simmering water, then drained and served hot in winter or cold in summer with a dipping sauce. Somen noodles are delicate, thin white Japanese noodles made from wheat flour, tied in bundles and held together with a paper band. Udon noodles are made from wheat flour and water. They are usually round, but can also be flat and are available fresh, precooked or dried from Oriental stores.

Nori
Dried seaweed is sold in paper-thin sheets which are dark green to black in colour and almost transparent in places. It is toasted and then used as a wrapping for sushi.

Onion seeds
Black, triangular seeds that are widely used in pickles and to flavour vegetable curries.

Oyster sauce
A thickish, slightly sweet and salty brown-coloured sauce made from oyster extract, soy sauce, sugar and vinegar. It is used to flavour meat, fish and vegetable dishes. A vegetarian version made from a mushroom base is also available.

Chapatis, and other Indian breads, are made from a special wholemeal flour.

Pak choi
Has large, green, spoon-shaped leaves and thick stalks. Also known as Chinese celery cabbage.

Palm sugar
Strongly flavoured, hard brown sugar made from the sap of the coconut palm tree. Soft, dark brown sugar will substitute if you cannot find it in Asian stores.

Peppercorns
One of the spices used to flavour curries. Good used freshly ground or crushed in recipes where black pepper is called for.

Basmati rice is traditionally grown in the foothills of the Himalayan mountains. It is delicious flavoured with cardamom pods.

Pickles
Pickled vegetables (tsukemono) are often served with rice dishes. Fresh root ginger is also pickled in various strengths of flavour.

Pomegranate seeds
These can be extracted from fresh pomegranates or bought in jars from Asian stores and give a delicious tangy flavour.

Red bean paste
Made from red kidney beans and sugar and used as a dip or spread on pancakes served with Peking Duck.

Rice vinegar
A pale vinegar that has a distinctive, delicate flavour.

Rice wine
Made from fermented glutinous, sticky rice, this golden wine is used for both drinking and cooking.

Saffron
The world's most expensive spice is the dried stigmas of the saffron crocus, which is native to Asia Minor. To produce 450g/1 lb of saffron requires 60,000 stigmas, but only a small quantity of saffron is needed to flavour and colour a dish. It is sold in strands and in powder form.

Sake
Japanese rice wine. It is not necessary to use expensive sake for cooking. Sake is drunk hot or chilled.

Sashimi
Slices of raw fish sushi used in Japanese cuisine.

Sesame oil
A nutty-flavoured oil extracted from toasted sesame seeds.

Sesame seeds
Black or white, these are available roasted or plain. Toast the plain seeds before using.

Seven-flavour spice or pepper
A chilli-based spice made of hemp, poppy, rape and sesame seeds, tangerine peel and anise-pepper leaves. It is used as a seasoning or condiment for noodle dishes and is available from Japanese food shops. Also known as sci-chimi.

Shallots
Thai shallots have a lovely pinkish-purple colour and are used widely in Thai cuisine instead of onions.

Shiitake mushrooms
The most popular mushroom in Japan, these have a good flavour, especially if dried. Soaking water from dried shiitake makes a good stock.

Shiratama-ko
Rice flour made from glutinous short grain rice with a high starch content.

Shiso leaves
A Japanese herb similar to basil.

Soy sauce
An essential ingredient in Asian cooking, particularly stir-fries and noodle dishes, soy sauce is made from fermented soya beans and ranges in colour from pale to dark, the lighter having more flavour than the sweeter dark variety.

Star anise
A spice used in Chinese dishes. It comes in the form of a dried, star-shaped seed pod that is usually added to braised and simmered dishes to give them an aniseed-like flavour.

Enoki mushrooms are delicious eaten raw.

Sushi
Different varieties of fresh uncooked fish pressed on rice.

Sushi vinegar
A seasoned and sweetened vinegar product for sushi.

Szechuan peppercorns
Used in Chinese dishes, these are reddish-brown in colour, and have a spicier, although less hot flavour than black peppercorns.

Tamarind
An acidic tropical fruit that resembles a bean pod, used in Thai cooking. It is usually sold dried or pulped. To make tamarind juice, take 25g/1oz of tamarind or about 2 stock cube-size

pieces and leave to soak in 150ml/¼ pint/⅔ cup of warm water for about 10 minutes. Squeeze out as much tamarind juice as possible by pressing all the liquid through a sieve.

Terasi
Shrimp paste made from fermented prawns and salt. Sold in blocks.

Tofu
Also known as bean curd or dofu, this is a soya bean product valued for its high protein content. It is useful in a vegetarian diet; it is also a good source of calcium and iron. There are several types, including soft or firm tofu, silken tofu, grilled tofu and dried tofu. Deep-fried tofu is sold ready-made in Japanese shops.

Thick, glossy, dark green banana leaves are widely used to line steamers or to wrap food prior to grilling or baking.

Toor dhal
A shiny split yellow lentil, toor dhal is similar in size to chana dhal.

Turmeric
A bright yellow, bitter-tasting spice sold ground. It is used mainly for colour rather than flavour.

Umeboshi
Small red pickled plums with a sharp and salty taste. They are considered a preservative and used to fill rice balls.

Urid dhal
Also known as black gram, this lentil is similar in size to moong dhal and is available either with the blackish hull retained or removed.

Vinegar
Thais use a mild, plain white vinegar. The Japanese use rice vinegar, a light and mild vinegar.

Wakame
Vacuum-packed or dried seaweed, for soups and salads.

Wasasbi
Green horseradish which tastes extremely hot. Available as a paste or a powder, to which water is added.

Wonton wrappers
Small square sheets rolled from egg-noodle dough, these are available in packets from Chinese food markets.

Yellow bean sauce
This is made from salted, fermented soya beans and added to flavour many savoury Asian dishes.

BASIC RECIPES

There are a few spice mixtures and stocks that form the basis of Asian cooking. They are not difficult or time-consuming to make and can be stored for weeks and used when needed. Ready-made versions are readily available but it is worth spending the time needed to produce a fresh, authentic version.

HOME-MADE GARAM MASALA

Garam masala is a mixture of spices that is used to flavour many Indian dishes. It can be made from freshly ground spices at home or bought ready-made. A typical mixture might include cumin seeds, peppercorns, cloves, cinnamon, bay leaves and nutmeg. In some versions, black cardamom pods and fenugreek seeds are added.

INGREDIENTS
7.5 cm/3 in piece cinnamon
stick
2 bay leaves
5 ml/1 tsp black cumin seeds
5 ml/1 tsp whole cloves
5 ml/1 tsp black peppercorns
¼ nutmeg, grated

1 Break the cinnamon sticks into pieces. Crumble the bay leaves.

2 Heat a small frying pan over a medium heat, then add the bay leaves and all the spices except the nutmeg.

3 Dry-fry until the spices turn a shade darker and emit a roasted aroma, stirring or shaking the pan frequently to prevent burning.

4 Leave to cool. Place all the ingredients in a spice mill or electric coffee grinder and grind to a fine powder. Store in a small jar with a tight-fitting lid for up to 2 months.

THAI RED CURRY PASTE

All curry making begins with the curry paste. Although traditionally made with a pestle and mortar, a blender or food processor produces a delicious paste within seconds.

INGREDIENTS
2.5 cm/1 in piece fresh root
*   ginger, chopped*
4 shallots, finely sliced
4-6 garlic cloves, chopped
4 lemon grass stalks, peeled
*   and chopped*
4 fresh red chillies, seeded
*   and chopped*
20 ml/4 tsp coriander seeds
10 ml/2 tsp cumin seeds
10 ml/2 tsp hot paprika
1.5 ml/¹/₄ tsp ground turmeric
2.5ml/¹/₂ tsp salt
grated rind and juice of 2 limes
15 ml/1 tbsp vegetable oil

1 Heat a small frying pan over a medium heat and add the coriander and cumin seeds. Toss them in the pan until the spices turn a shade darker and emit a roasted aroma. Leave to cool.

2 Peel and chop the ginger, shallots and garlic. Peel and finely chop the lemon grass. Peel and roughly chop the chillies as directed overleaf.

3 Place all the ingredients in a blender or food processor and process together to form a smooth paste.

4 Store in a screw-top jar for up to 1 month in the fridge and use as required.

BASIC TECHNIQUES

For the ingredients to cook quickly and still absorb the taste of the oil and flavouring, they should be cut into small uniform pieces with as many cut surfaces as possible exposed to the heat. Careful cutting also enhances the visual appeal of a dish — a factor that is very important in Asian cuisines.

CHOPPING CHILLIES

The fire in chillies comes from the seeds, so discard them for a milder flavour. Chillies contain an oil that can irritate the skin and eyes. Wash hands thoroughly and avoid touching the face or eyes after cutting chillies, or wear rubber gloves.

1 Slice the chillies, and then remove the seeds. It is advisable to wear rubber gloves to protect your skin.

2 Finely chop the chillies and use as required.

PEELING AND CHOPPING LEMON GRASS

Aromatic lemon grass can be bought from Oriental food stores and some larger supermarkets.

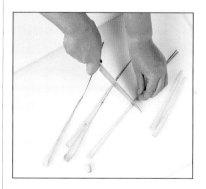 

1 Cut off and discard the dry leafy tops, leaving about 15cm/6in of stalk. Peel away any tough outer layers from the lemon grass.

2 Lay the lemon grass on a board. Set a cleaver or chef's knife on top and strike it firmly with your fist; this helps to extract maximum flavour. Cut across the lemon grass to make thin slices, then continue chopping until fine.

CHOPPING MEAT FOR STIR-FRYING

The speed of this method of cooking requires meat to be cut as thinly as possible. Always use a sharp bladed knife.

1 Beef is always cut across the grain otherwise it will become tough; pork, lamb and chicken can be cut either along or across the grain.

2 Placing the meat in the freezer for about 1 hour beforehand makes it easier to cut paper-thin slices.

CUTTING JULIENNE STRIPS

After cooking, julienne strips of vegetables can be tied in individual bundles with a chive and used as an appealing and edible garnish.

1 Peel the vegetable and use a large knife to cut it into 5cm/2in lengths. Cut a thin sliver from one side of the first piece so that it will sit flat on the board.

2 Cut each strip, lengthwise, into thin wedges.

3 Stack the slices and then cut through them to make fine strips (*above*).

Appetizers

Appetizers are a Western phenomenon. While Western cultures begin their meals with a soup or savoury dish, Asian countries serve one large course, combining soups, rice, noodles, vegetables, protein and pulses. The importance here is to harmoniously balance flavours, colours, cooking methods and ingredients and then enjoy the results in any order.

For Western consumers, the typical Asian dishes offer many delicious titbits that are perfect for appetizers. For example, delicate quail's eggs are marbled in lapsang souchong tea for a fragrant and attractive appetizer from China. For a more substantial start, Pan-steamed Mussels with Thai Herbs takes an already delicious seafood dish and brings it alive with the tangy flavour of lemon grass and the spice of red chillies.

Familiar soups based on chicken or vegetables also get a twist with the addition of flavourful Asian ingredients including coriander, root ginger, kaffir lime leaves, soy sauce, dashi and tamarind.

CHICKEN AND ALMOND SOUP

This soup makes an excellent appetizer and, served with Naan Bread, will also make a satisfying lunch or supper dish.

INGREDIENTS
75g/3oz/6 tbsp unsalted butter
1 leek, chopped
2.5ml/½ tsp sliced fresh root ginger
75g/3oz/1 cup ground almonds
5ml/1 tsp salt
2.5ml/½ tsp crushed black peppercorns
1 fresh green chilli, chopped
115g/4oz chicken, skinned, boned and cubed
1 carrot, sliced
50g/2oz/½ cup frozen peas
15ml/1 tbsp chopped fresh coriander
450ml/¾ pint/scant 2 cups water
250ml/8fl oz/1 cup single cream
4 fresh coriander sprigs, to garnish

SERVES 4

1 Melt the butter in a large karahi or deep round-bottomed frying pan and sauté the leek with the ginger until soft.

2 Lower the heat and add the ground almonds, salt, peppercorns, chilli, chicken, carrot and peas. Fry for about 10 minutes or until the chicken is completely cooked, stirring constantly. Add the chopped fresh coriander.

3 Remove the pan from the heat and allow to cool slightly. Transfer the mixture to a food processor or blender and process for about 1½ minutes. Pour in the water and blend for a further 30 seconds.

4 Pour the puréed mixture back into the karahi or frying pan and bring slowly to the boil, stirring occasionally. Once the soup has boiled, lower the heat and gradually stir in the single cream. Cook the soup, without bringing to the boil, for a further 2 minutes, stirring occasionally, until the cream is just heated through.

5 To serve, transfer the soup to warmed individual bowls, garnish each one with a fresh coriander sprig and serve immediately.

SPICY CHICKEN AND MUSHROOM SOUP

he combination of hot spices and cream makes this soup a perfect warming dish for a winter's night.

INGREDIENTS

225g/8oz chicken, skinned and boned
75g/3oz/6 tbsp unsalted butter
½ garlic clove, crushed
5ml/1 tsp garam masala
5ml/1 tsp crushed black peppercorns
5ml/1 tsp salt
1.5ml/¼ tsp ground nutmeg
1 leek, sliced
75g/3oz/1 cup mushrooms, sliced
50g/2oz/⅓ cup sweetcorn
300ml/½ pint/1¼ cups water
250ml/8fl oz/1 cup single cream
15ml/1 tbsp chopped fresh coriander
*5ml/1 tsp crushed dried red chillies
(optional), to garnish*

SERVES 4

1 Using a sharp knife, cut the chicken pieces into very fine strips. Melt the butter in a saucepan and add the garlic and garam masala. Lower the heat and add the peppercorns, salt and nutmeg. Finally, add the strips of chicken, sliced leek, mushrooms and sweetcorn and cook for 5–7 minutes or until the chicken is cooked through, stirring constantly.

2 Remove the saucepan from the heat and allow the chicken mixture to cool slightly. Transfer three-quarters of the mixture to a food processor or blender. Add the water and process for about 1 minute until smooth.

3 Stir the purée back into the saucepan with the rest of the mixture and bring to the boil over a moderate heat. Lower the heat and stir in the cream.

4 Add the fresh coriander, then taste for seasoning. Serve hot, garnished with the crushed red chillies, if using.

PRAWNS WITH POMEGRANATE SEEDS

King prawns are the best choice for this Balti dish. It makes an impressive appetizer for a dinner party, and is delicious served with a mixed salad.

INGREDIENTS

5ml/1 tsp crushed garlic
5ml/1 tsp sliced fresh root ginger
5ml/1 tsp coarsely ground pomegranate seeds
5ml/1 tsp ground coriander
5ml/1 tsp salt
5ml/1 tsp chilli powder
30ml/2 tbsp tomato purée
60ml/4 tbsp water
45ml/3 tbsp chopped fresh coriander
30ml/2 tbsp corn oil
12 large cooked prawns
1 onion, sliced into rings

SERVES 4–6

1 Put the garlic, ginger, pomegranate seeds, ground coriander, salt, chilli powder, tomato purée, water and 30ml/2 tbsp of the fresh coriander into a bowl. Pour in the oil and blend thoroughly.

2 Peel the prawns. Using a sharp knife, make a small slit at the back of each prawn, then gently open them out to make a butterfly shape.

3 Add the prawns to the spice mixture, coating them well. Cover and leave to marinate for about 2 hours.

4 Cut four squares of foil, each about 20 × 20 cm/8 × 8 in. Preheat the oven to 230°C/450°F/Gas 8. Place three prawns and a few onion rings on each square of foil, garnishing them with a little fresh coriander, and fold up into little packages. Bake the prawns for about 12–15 minutes and open up the foil packages to serve.

OPPOSITE: A mixed salad (TOP) is delicious with Prawns with Pomegranate Seeds (CENTRE) and Grilled Prawns (BOTTOM)

GRILLED PRAWNS

Prawns are delicious grilled, especially when they are flavoured with spices.

INGREDIENTS

60ml/4 tbsp lemon juice
5ml/1 tsp salt
5ml/1 tsp chilli powder
1 garlic clove, crushed
7.5ml/1½ tsp soft light brown sugar
45ml/3 tbsp corn oil
30ml/2 tbsp chopped fresh coriander
18 large peeled, cooked prawns
1 fresh green chilli, sliced
1 tomato, sliced
1 small onion, cut into rings
lemon wedges, to garnish

SERVES 4–6

1 Combine the lemon juice, salt, chilli powder, garlic, sugar, corn oil and fresh coriander in a bowl. Add the prawns, coating them well. Cover and leave to marinate for about 1 hour.

2 Place the green chilli, tomato slices and onion rings in a flameproof dish. Add the prawn mixture and cook under a preheated very hot grill for about 10–15 minutes, basting several times. Serve at once, garnished with the lemon wedges.

HOT AND SOUR PRAWN SOUP WITH LEMON GRASS

 his is a classic seafood soup – *Tom Yam Goong* – and is probably the most popular of Thai soups.

INGREDIENTS

450g/1lb king prawns (raw or cooked)
1 litre/1¾ pints/4 cups chicken stock or water
3 lemon grass stalks
10 kaffir lime leaves, torn in half
225g/8oz can straw mushrooms, drained
45ml/3 tbsp fish sauce
50ml/2fl oz/¼ cup lime juice
30ml/2 tbsp chopped spring onions
15ml/1 tbsp coriander leaves
4 red chillies, seeded and chopped

SERVES 4–6

1 Shell and de-vein the prawns and set aside. Rinse the prawn shells, place in a large saucepan with the stock or water and bring to the boil.

2 Bruise the lemon grass stalks with the blunt edge of a chopping knife and add them to the stock together with half of the lime leaves. Simmer gently for 5–6 minutes, until the stalks change colour and the stock is fragrant.

3 Strain the stock, return to the saucepan and reheat. Add the mushrooms and prawns, then cook for a few minutes, or until the prawns turn pink if raw.

4 Stir in the fish sauce, lime juice, spring onions, coriander, chillies and the rest of the lime leaves. Taste; adjust the flavours. It should be sour, salty, spicy and hot.

SPINACH AND BEAN CURD SOUP

 n extremely delicate and mild-flavoured soup that can be used to counterbalance the heat from a hot Thai curry.

INGREDIENTS
30ml/2 tbsp dried shrimps
1 litre/1¾ pints/4 cups chicken stock
225g/8oz fresh bean curd, drained and cut into 2cm/¾in cubes
30ml/2 tbsp fish sauce
350g/12oz fresh spinach leaves, thoroughly washed
freshly ground black pepper
2 spring onions, finely sliced, to garnish

SERVES 4–6

1 Rinse and drain the dried shrimps. Combine the shrimps with the chicken stock in a saucepan and bring to the boil.

2 Add the bean curd and simmer for about 5 minutes. Season with fish sauce and black pepper to taste.

3 Tear the spinach leaves into bite-size pieces and add to the soup. Cook for another 1–2 minutes.

4 Remove the soup from the heat, ladle into bowls and sprinkle over the finely sliced spring onions, to garnish.

THAI CHICKEN SOUP

 spicy light soup sweetened with coconut and crunchy peanut butter for added bite.

INGREDIENTS
15ml/1 tbsp vegetable oil
1 garlic clove, finely chopped
2 x 175g/6oz boned chicken breasts,
skinned and chopped
2.5ml/½ tsp ground turmeric
1.5ml/¼ tsp hot chilli powder
75g/3oz creamed coconut
900ml/1½ pints/3¾ cups hot
chicken stock
dash of lemon juice
30ml/2 tbsp crunchy peanut butter
50g/2oz/1 cup thread egg noodles, broken
into small pieces
15ml/1 tbsp spring onions,
finely chopped
15ml/1 tbsp chopped fresh coriander
salt and freshly ground black pepper
30ml/2 tbsp desiccated coconut and
½ fresh red chilli, seeded and finely
chopped, to garnish

SERVES 4

1 Heat the oil in a large pan and fry the garlic for 1 minute. Add the chicken and spices and stir-fry for a further 3–4 minutes.

2 Crumble the creamed coconut into the hot chicken stock and stir until dissolved. Pour this mixture on to the chicken and add the lemon juice, peanut butter and egg noodles.

3 Cover and simmer for about 15 minutes. Add the spring onions and fresh coriander, then season well with salt and freshly ground black pepper and cook for a further 5 minutes.

4 Meanwhile, place the coconut and chopped chilli in a small frying pan and heat for about 3 minutes, stirring frequently, until the coconut is lightly browned.

5 Pour the soup into individual bowls and sprinkle with the fried coconut and chopped chilli.

GOLDEN POUCHES

T hese crisp pouches from Thailand are delicious served as an appetizer or as finger food at a party.

INGREDIENTS

115g/4oz minced pork
115g/4oz crab meat
2–3 wood ears, soaked and chopped
15ml/1 tbsp chopped coriander
5ml/1 tsp chopped garlic
30ml/2 tbsp chopped spring onions
1 egg
15ml/1 tbsp fish sauce
5ml/1 tsp soy sauce
pinch of granulated sugar
20 wonton wrappers
20 long chives, blanched (optional)
oil, for deep frying
freshly ground black pepper
plum or sweet chilli sauce, to serve

MAKES ABOUT 20

1 In a mixing bowl, combine the pork, crab meat, wood ears, coriander, garlic, spring onions and egg. Mix well and season with fish sauce, soy sauce, sugar and freshly ground black pepper.

2 Take a wonton wrapper and place it on a flat surface. Put a heaped teaspoonful of filling in the centre of the wrapper, then pull up the edges of the pastry around the filling.

3 Pinch together to seal. If you like, you can go a step further and tie it with a long chive. Repeat with the remaining pork mixture and wonton wrappers.

4 Heat the oil in a wok or deep-fat fryer. Fry the wontons in batches until they are crisp and golden brown. Drain on kitchen paper and serve immediately with either a plum or sweet chilli sauce.

STEAMED SEAFOOD PACKETS

Very neat and delicate, these steamed packets make an excellent starter or a light lunch. You can find glossy, green banana leaves in oriental food shops.

INGREDIENTS
225g/8oz crab meat
50g/2oz shelled prawns, chopped
6 water chestnuts, chopped
30ml/2 tbsp chopped bamboo shoots
15ml/1 tbsp chopped spring onion
5ml/1 tsp chopped root ginger
15ml/1 tbsp soy sauce
15ml/1 tbsp fish sauce
12 rice sheets
banana leaves
oil, for brushing
2 spring onions, shredded
2 red chillies, seeded and sliced,
and coriander leaves, to garnish

SERVES 4

1 Combine the crab meat, chopped prawns, water chestnuts, bamboo shoots, chopped spring onion and ginger in a bowl. Mix well, then add the soy sauce and fish sauce. Stir until blended.

2 Take a rice sheet and dip it in warm water. Place it on a flat surface and leave for a few seconds to soften.

3 Place a spoonful of the filling in the centre of the sheet and fold into a square packet. Repeat with the rest of the rice sheets and seafood mixture.

4 Use banana leaves to line a steamer, then brush them with oil. Place the packets, seam-side down, on the leaves and steam over a high heat for 6–8 minutes or until the filling is cooked.

5 Transfer on to a plate and serve, garnished with the shredded spring onions, sliced chillies and coriander.

COOK'S TIP
The seafood packets will spread out when steamed, so be sure to space them well apart to prevent them sticking together.

PAN-STEAMED MUSSELS WITH THAI HERBS

nother simple dish to prepare. The lemon grass adds a refreshing tang to the mussels.

INGREDIENTS
1kg/2¼lb mussels, cleaned and beards removed
2 lemon grass stalks, finely chopped
4 shallots, chopped
4 kaffir lime leaves, roughly torn
2 red chillies, seeded and sliced
15ml/1 tbsp fish sauce
30ml/2 tbsp lime juice
2 spring onions, chopped, and coriander leaves, to garnish

SERVES 4–6

1 Place all the ingredients, except for the spring onions and coriander, in a large saucepan and stir thoroughly.

2 Cover and steam for 5–7 minutes, shaking the saucepan occasionally, until the mussels open. Discard any mussels that do not open.

3 Transfer the cooked mussels to a warmed serving dish.

4 Garnish the mussels with chopped spring onions and coriander leaves. Serve immediately.

FISH CAKES WITH CUCUMBER RELISH

These wonderful small fish cakes are a familiar and popular appetizer, usually accompanied by Thai beer.

INGREDIENTS
300g/11oz white fish fillet, such as cod,
cut into chunks
30ml/2 tbsp red curry paste
1 egg
30ml/2 tbsp fish sauce
5ml/1 tsp granulated sugar
30ml/2 tbsp cornflour
3 kaffir lime leaves, shredded
15ml/1 tbsp chopped coriander
50g/2oz green beans, finely sliced
oil, for frying
Chinese mustard cress, to garnish

FOR THE CUCUMBER RELISH
60ml/4 tbsp Thai coconut
or rice vinegar
60ml/4 tbsp water
50g/2oz sugar
1 head of pickled garlic
1 cucumber, quartered and sliced
4 shallots, finely sliced
15ml/1 tbsp finely chopped root ginger
2 red chillies, seeded and finely sliced

MAKES ABOUT 12

1 To make the cucumber relish, bring the vinegar, water and sugar to the boil. Stir until the sugar dissolves, then remove from the heat and cool.

2 Combine the rest of the relish ingredients together in a bowl and pour over the vinegar mixture.

3 Combine the fish, curry paste and egg in a food processor and process well. Transfer the mixture to a bowl, add the rest of the ingredients, except for the oil and garnish, and mix well.

4 Mould and shape the mixture into cakes about 5cm/2in in diameter and 5mm/¼in thick.

5 Heat the oil in a wok or deep-fat fryer. Fry the fish cakes, a few at a time, for about 4–5 minutes or until golden brown. Remove and drain on kitchen paper. Garnish with Chinese mustard cress and serve with the cucumber relish.

HANOI BEEF AND NOODLE SOUP

his fragrant North Vietnamese soup, traditionally eaten for breakfast, makes a filling starter.

INGREDIENTS
1 onion
1.5kg/3–3½lb beef shank with bones
2.5cm/1in fresh root ginger
1 star anise
1 bay leaf
2 whole cloves
2.5ml/½ tsp fennel seeds
1 piece of cassia bark or cinnamon stick
3 litres/5 pints/12½ cups water
fish sauce, to taste
juice of 1 lime
150g/5oz fillet steak
450g/1lb fresh flat rice noodles

ACCOMPANIMENTS
1 small red onion, sliced into rings
115g/4oz beansprouts
2 red chillies, seeded and sliced
3 spring onions, finely sliced
handful of coriander leaves
lime wedges

SERVES 4–6

1 Cut the onion in half. Grill under a high heat, cut side up, until the exposed sides are caramelized, and deep brown. Set aside.

2 Cut the bones from the meat, and chop into large chunks. Place the meat and the bones into a large saucepan or stock pot. Add the caramelized onion with the ginger, star anise, bay leaf, cloves, fennel seeds and cassia bark or cinnamon stick.

3 Add the water, bring to the boil, reduce the heat and **simmer gently for 2–3 hours, skimming off** the fat and white froth from time to time.

4 Using a slotted spoon, remove the meat from the stock; when cool enough to handle, cut into small pieces, discarding the bones. Strain the stock and return to the pan or stock pot together with the meat. Bring back to the boil and season with the fish sauce and lime juice.

5 Slice the fillet steak very thinly and then chill until required. Place the accompaniments in separate bowls so that everyone can help themselves.

6 Cook the noodles in a large saucepan of boiling water until just tender. Drain and divide among individual serving bowls. Arrange the thinly sliced steak over the noodles and pour the hot stock on top.

VIETNAMESE SPRING ROLLS

runchy spring rolls are the perfect starter, complemented here by *nuoc cham* sauce.

INGREDIENTS
6 dried Chinese mushrooms, soaked
225g/8oz lean ground pork
115g/4oz uncooked prawns, peeled,
deveined and chopped
115g/4oz white crabmeat, picked over
1 carrot, shredded
50g/2oz cellophane noodles, soaked in
water, drained and cut into short lengths
4 spring onions, finely sliced
2 garlic cloves, finely chopped
30ml/2 tbsp fish sauce
juice of 1 lime
freshly ground black pepper
25 x 10cm/4in Vietnamese rice sheets
oil, for deep frying

FOR THE SAUCE
2 garlic cloves, finely chopped
30ml/2 tbsp white wine vinegar
juice of 1 lime
30ml/2 tbsp sugar
120ml/4fl oz/½ cup fish sauce
120ml/4fl oz/½ cup water
2 red chillies, seeded and chopped

MAKES 25

1 Drain the mushrooms. Remove and discard the stems and slice the caps into a bowl. Add the pork, prawns, crabmeat, carrot, noodles, spring onions and garlic.

2 Season with the fish sauce, lime juice and pepper. Set the mixture aside for 30 minutes to allow the flavours to blend.

3 Meanwhile make the *nuoc cham* sauce. Mix together the garlic, vinegar, lime juice, sugar, fish sauce, water and chillies in a serving bowl, then cover and set aside.

4 Assemble the spring rolls. Brush a rice sheet with warm water until pliable. Place 10ml/2 tsp of the filling near the edge of the sheet. Fold the sides over the filling, fold in the two ends, then roll up, sealing the ends with a little water.

5 Make more rolls until all the filling is used up. Then heat the oil for deep frying to 180°C/350°F or until a cube of dry bread added to the oil browns in 30–45 seconds. Add the rolls, a few at a time, and fry until golden brown and crisp. Drain on kitchen paper. Serve hot, garnished with lettuce, cucumber, radish and coriander, if desired. Offer the *nuoc cham* sauce in a separate bowl.

PORK SATAY

Originating in Indonesia, satay are skewers of meat marinated with spices and grilled quickly over charcoal. You can make them with chicken, beef or lamb.

INGREDIENTS
450g/1lb lean pork
5ml/1 tsp grated root ginger
1 lemon grass stalk, finely chopped
3 garlic cloves, finely chopped
15ml/1 tbsp medium curry paste
5ml/1 tsp ground cumin
5ml/1 tsp ground turmeric
60ml/4 tbsp coconut cream
30ml/2 tbsp fish sauce
5ml/1 tsp granulated sugar
20 wooden satay skewers
oil, for brushing
sprigs of mint, to garnish

FOR THE SATAY SAUCE
250ml/8fl oz/1 cup coconut milk
30ml/2 tbsp red curry paste
75g/3oz crunchy peanut butter
120ml/4fl oz/½ cup chicken stock
45ml/3 tbsp brown sugar
30ml/2 tbsp tamarind juice
15ml/1 tbsp fish sauce
2.5ml/½ tsp salt

MAKES ABOUT 20

1 Cut the pork thinly into 5cm/2in strips. Mix together the ginger, lemon grass, garlic, medium curry paste, cumin, turmeric, coconut cream, fish sauce and sugar.

2 Pour over the pork and leave to marinate for about 2 hours.

3 Meanwhile, make the sauce. Heat the coconut milk over a medium heat, then add the red curry paste, peanut butter, chicken stock and sugar.

4 Cook and stir until smooth, for about 5–6 minutes. Add the tamarind juice, fish sauce and salt to taste.

5 Thread the meat on to skewers. Brush with oil and grill over charcoal or under a preheated grill for 3–4 minutes on each side, turning occasionally, until cooked. Garnish with mint and serve with the satay sauce.

TAMARIND AND VEGETABLE SOUP

 ayur Assam is a colourful and refreshing soup from Jakarta with more than a hint of sharpness.

INGREDIENTS
5 shallots or 1 medium red onion, sliced
3 garlic cloves, crushed
2.5cm/1in lengkuas, *peeled and sliced*
1–2 fresh red chillies, seeded and sliced
25g/1oz raw peanuts
1cm/½in cube terasi, *prepared*
1.2 litres/2 pints/5 cups
well-flavoured stock
50–75g/2 –3oz salted peanuts,
lightly crushed
15–30ml/1–2 tbsp dark brown sugar
5ml/1 tsp tamarind pulp, soaked in
75ml/5 tbsp warm water for 15 minutes
salt
1 fresh green chilli, sliced, to garnish

FOR THE VEGETABLES
1 chayote, thinly peeled, seeds removed,
flesh finely sliced
115g/4oz French beans, trimmed and
finely sliced
50g/2oz/¼ cup sweetcorn kernels
handful green leaves, such as watercress,
rocket or Chinese leaves, finely shredded

SERVES 4

1 Prepare the spice paste by grinding the shallots or onion, garlic, *lengkuas,* chillies, raw peanuts and *terasi* to a paste in a food processor or with a pestle and mortar.

2 Pour in some of the stock to moisten and then pour this mixture into a pan or wok, adding the rest of the stock. Cook for 15 minutes with the lightly crushed peanuts and sugar.

3 Strain the tamarind, discarding the seeds, and reserve the juice.

4 About 5 minutes before serving, add the chayote slices, beans and sweetcorn to the soup and cook fairly rapidly. At the last minute, add the green leaves and salt to taste.

5 Add the tamarind juice and taste for seasoning. Serve, garnished with slices of green chilli.

GARLIC MUSHROOMS

T ofu is high in protein and very low in fat, so it is a very useful food to keep handy for quick and healthy dishes like this one from China.

INGREDIENTS
8 large open-cup mushrooms
3 spring onions, sliced lengthways
1 garlic clove, crushed
30ml/2 tbsp oyster sauce
275g/10oz carton marinated tofu, cut into small dice
200g/7oz can sweetcorn, drained
10ml/2 tsp sesame oil
salt and ground black pepper
spring onion strips, to garnish

SERVES 4

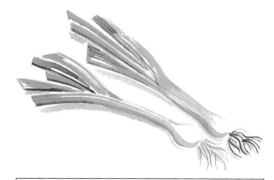

COOK'S TIP
If you prefer, omit the oyster sauce and use light soy sauce instead.

1 Preheat the oven to 200°C/400°F/Gas 6. Set aside the mushroom cups and finely chop the stalks. Place the stalks in a bowl, add the spring onions and garlic and pour over the oyster sauce. Stir to mix.

2 Dry the marinated tofu and add it with the sweetcorn to the mushroom mixture, season with salt and pepper, then stir to combine.

3 Place the mushroom cups, open-side up, on a plate or chopping board and divide the stuffing mixture among them.

4 Brush the edges of the mushrooms with the oil. Arrange the mushrooms in a baking dish and bake for 12–15 minutes, until the mushrooms are just tender, then serve garnished with the spring onion strips.

MARBLED QUAIL'S EGGS

Hard-boiled quail's eggs reboiled in smoky China tea assume a pretty marbled effect. Dip them into a fragrant spicy salt and hand them round with drinks, or serve them as a starter. Szechuan peppercorns can be bought from oriental food shops.

INGREDIENTS
12 quail's eggs
600ml/1 pint/2½ cups strong lapsang souchong tea
15ml/1 tbsp dark soy sauce
15ml/1 tbsp dry sherry
2 whole star anise
curly endive, ground Szechuan peppercorns and sea salt, to serve

SERVES 4–6

1 Place the quail's eggs in a saucepan of cold water and bring to the boil. Time them for 2 minutes from the moment when the water comes to the boil.

2 Transfer the eggs from the pan to a colander and run them under cold water to cool. Tap the shells all over so they are crazed, but do not peel the eggs.

COOK'S TIP
Szechuan peppercorns are dried reddish brown berries from a shrub native to Szechuan. They are not so hot as the true peppercorn, but have a numbing effect and a distinctive aroma. They are roasted, ground, and the husks discarded before use.

3 In a large saucepan, bring the tea to the boil, then add the soy sauce, sherry and star anise. Add the eggs and boil again for about 15 minutes, partially covered, so the liquid does not boil dry.

4 Remove the eggs from the pan. When they are cool, peel and arrange on a small platter lined with curly endive.

5 Mix the ground Szechuan peppercorns with an equal quantity of salt and place the mixture in a small dish to serve with the eggs.

PRAWN AND EGG-KNOT SOUP

There are no set main courses in Japan and all dishes are eaten together. Soup is also eaten for breakfast, when it is typically served with seaweed and a soft-boiled egg.

INGREDIENTS
800ml/1¹/₃ pints/3¹/₂ cups kombu and
bonito stock or instant dashi
5ml/1 tsp usukuchi soy sauce
salt
1 spring onion, thinly sliced,
to garnish

FOR THE PRAWN SHINJO BALLS
200g/7oz raw large prawns, shelled,
thawed if frozen
65g/2¹/₂oz cod fillet, skinned
5ml/1 tsp egg white
5ml/1 tsp sake or dry white wine, plus an
extra dash
22.5ml/4¹/₂ tsp cornflour or potato starch
2–3 drops soy sauce

FOR THE OMELETTE
1 egg, beaten
dash of mirin
oil, for cooking

SERVES 4

1 Remove the black vein running down the back of the prawns. Process the prawns, cod, egg white, the sake or wine, cornflour or potato starch, soy sauce and a pinch of salt together in a food processor or blender to make a sticky paste. Alternatively, finely chop the prawns and cod, crush them with the knife's blade and then pound them well in a mortar with a pestle, adding the remaining ingredients.

2 Shape the mixture into four balls and steam for 10 minutes over a high heat. Soak the spring onion in cold water for 5 minutes, then drain.

3 Mix the egg with a pinch of salt and the mirin. Heat a little oil in a frying pan and pour in the egg, tilting the pan to coat it evenly. When the egg has set, turn the omelette over and cook for 30 seconds. Leave to cool.

4 Cut the cooked omelette into long strips, each about 2cm/³/₄in wide. Knot each strip once, place in a strainer and rinse with hot water to remove any excess oil. Bring the stock to the boil and add the *usukuchi* soy sauce, a pinch of salt and a dash of sake or wine.

5 Divide the prawn balls and the egg knots among four serving bowls. Pour in the soup, sprinkle with the spring onion and serve immediately.

SHIITAKE MUSHROOM AND EGG SOUP

O*sumashi* means "clear soup". This Japanese recipe goes particularly well with any sushi, as its delicate flavour complements rather than overpowers the flavour of the fish.

INGREDIENTS
600ml/1 pint/2½ cups kombu and bonito stock or instant dashi
4 shiitake mushrooms, stems removed, thinly sliced
5ml/1 tsp salt
10ml/2 tsp usukuchi *soy sauce*
5ml/1 tsp sake or dry white wine
2 size 4 eggs
½ punnet of cress, to garnish

SERVES 4

COOK'S TIP
Shiitake mushrooms can be used to make a delicious stock. Just use the water that you have used to soak them in if they are dried.

1 Bring the stock to the boil, add the shiitake mushrooms and simmer for about 1–2 minutes. Do not overcook.

2 Add the salt, *usukuchi* soy sauce and sake or wine. Then break the eggs into a bowl and stir well with chopsticks.

3 Pour the egg into the soup in a thin steady stream, in a circular motion – rather like drawing a spiral shape in the soup. To keep the soup clear, the heat must be high enough to set the egg as soon as it is added.

4 Simmer the soup for a few seconds until the eggs are cooked through. Use a pair of chopsticks to break up the egg in order to serve it equally among four bowls. Remove from the heat. Sprinkle with some cress and serve immediately.

MISO SOUP

This soup is one of the most commonly eaten dishes in Japan, and it is usually served with every meal. Every family has its unique recipe for this soup, with different combinations of ingredients.

INGREDIENTS
150g/5oz Japanese silken tofu,
10 x 5 x 3cm/4 x 2 x 1¼ in
800ml/1⅓ pints/3½ cups kombu and
bonito stock or instant dashi
10g/¼oz dried wakame seaweed
60ml/4 tbsp white or red miso paste
2 spring onions, chopped,
to garnish

SERVES 4

1 Cut the tofu into 1cm/½in cubes. Bring the stock to the boil and reduce the heat.

2 Add the wakame seaweed and simmer for 1–2 minutes.

3 Pour some soup into a bowl and add the miso paste, stirring until it dissolves, and then pour the mixture back into the pan.

4 Add the tofu and heat through for about 1 minute, then serve immediately, while still very hot. Garnish with the chopped spring onions.

COOK'S TIP
Reduce the heat when the stock boils as it loses flavour if boiled for too long. Similarly, cook the soup long enough to heat the ingredients.

PRAWN TEMPURA

Tempura is a delicate dish of savoury fritters in light batter. The secret is to use really cold water and to have the oil at the right temperature.

INGREDIENTS
8 raw tiger prawns, heads removed
oil, for deep frying
65g/2½ oz mooli, finely grated and drained, and a shiso leaf, to garnish

FOR THE TEMPURA DIP
200ml/7fl oz/scant 1 cup water
45ml/3 tbsp mirin
10g/¼oz bonito flakes
45ml/3 tbsp soy sauce

FOR THE TEMPURA BATTER
1 egg
90ml/6 tbsp iced water
75g/3oz/⅔ cup plain flour
2.5ml/½ tsp baking powder
2 ice cubes

SERVES 4

COOK'S TIP
Always use Japanese soy sauce in these recipes as Chinese soy sauce tastes much stronger.

---

1 Carefully shell the tiger prawns, leaving their tails on. Cut one-third of each tail off in a diagonal slit. Press out any excess water with your fingers to prevent it from seeping into the oil and spitting during the cooking process.

2 Make a shallow cut down the back of each prawn and remove the black intestinal vein.

3 Lay a prawn on its spine so that it is concave. Using a sharp knife, make three or four diagonal slits into the flesh, about two-thirds of the way in towards the spine, leaving all the pieces attached.

4 Repeat this process with the remaining prawns. This keeps them straight during cooking. Finally, flatten the prawns with your fingers.

5 To make the dip, put all the ingredients in a saucepan and bring to the boil. Remove from the heat, leave to cool, and then strain.

6 Slowly heat the oil for deep frying to 185°C/365°F. Start making the batter when the oil is getting warm.

7 Always make the batter just before you use it so that it is still very cold. Stir, but do not beat, the egg in a large bowl and set aside half for another use. Add the iced water, flour and baking powder all at once. Stir only two or three times, ignoring the lumps. Add the ice cubes.

8 Dust the prawns lightly with flour. Hold one by the tail, quickly coat it with batter and slowly lower it into the oil. Do not drop the prawn into the oil as the coating comes off.

9 Repeat with the remaining prawns, frying them until they rise to the surface of the oil and are crisp. Do not fry until they are golden. Cook a few prawns at a time and then drain them well. Pour the dip into four small bowls. Place the tempura on a plate, garnish with the mooli and shiso leaf and serve immediately.

SPINACH WITH BONITO FLAKES

T his is a cold side dish of lightly cooked spinach dressed with fine bonito flakes. A similar vegetarian side dish can be prepared by omitting the bonito flakes and marinating the spinach in kombu seaweed dashi and soy sauce.

INGREDIENTS
300g/11oz whole spinach, roots trimmed

FOR THE MARINADE
60ml/4 tbsp kombu and bonito stock or instant dashi
20ml/4 tsp usukuchi *soy sauce*
60ml/4 tbsp fine bonito flakes
(katsuo bushi)

SERVES 4

1 Wash the spinach thoroughly. Keeping the stems together, hold the leaves of the spinach and lower the stems into boiling water for 10 seconds before lowering the leaves into the water and boiling for about 1–2 minutes. Do not overcook the spinach.

2 Meanwhile, prepare a large bowl of cold water. Drain the spinach and soak it in the cold water for 1 minute to preserve its colour and remove any bitterness.

3 Drain the spinach and squeeze it well, holding the stems upwards and squeezing firmly down the length of the spinach leaves.

4 Mix the stock and soy sauce in a dish and marinate the spinach in this mixture for 10–15 minutes, turning it over once.

5 Squeeze the spinach lightly and cut it into 3–4cm/1¼ –1½in long pieces, reserving the marinade. Divide the spinach among four small bowls, arranging the pieces so that the cut edges face upwards. Sprinkle 15ml/1 tbsp bonito flakes and a little of the marinade over each portion, then serve immediately.

MOOLI WITH SESAME MISO SAUCE

This simple vegetable dish makes a good starter. The rice is added to keep the mooli white and to remove any bitterness from the vegetables.

INGREDIENTS
1 mooli, about 800g/1¾lb
15ml/1 tbsp rice, washed
salt, to taste
1 sheet kombu seaweed,
20 x 10cm/8 x 4in
punnet of cress, to garnish

FOR THE SESAME MISO SAUCE
75g/3oz/generous ⅓ cup each red and
white miso paste
60ml/4 tbsp mirin
30ml/2 tbsp sugar
20ml/4 tsp ground white sesame seeds

SERVES 4

1 Slice the mooli into 2cm/¾in thick slices, then peel off the skin. Wrap the rice in a piece of muslin or cheesecloth and tie with string, allowing room for the rice to expand during cooking. Place the mooli, rice bag and some salt in a pan, fill with water and bring to the boil. Simmer for 15 minutes. Gently drain the mooli and discard the rice.

2 Place the seaweed in a large pan, lay the mooli on top and fill with water. Bring to the boil, then simmer for 20 minutes.

3 Meanwhile, make the sauce. Mix the red and white miso pastes together in a saucepan. Add the mirin and sugar, simmer for 5–6 minutes, and make sure that you stir continuously. Remove from the heat and add the sesame seeds.

4 Arrange the mooli and seaweed in a large dish with their hot cooking stock. Sprinkle cress over the top. Serve the mooli on small plates with the sesame miso sauce poured over and garnished with some of the cress. The seaweed is used only to flavour the mooli and is not eaten.

SIMPLE ROLLED SUSHI

T o perfect the art of rolling sushi in seaweed, start with this simple form of rolled sushi known as *Hosomaki,* which is usually a slim roll with only one filling. You will need a bamboo mat *(makisu)* for the rolling process.

INGREDIENTS
6 sheets yaki-nori *seaweed*
gari *(ginger pickles), to garnish*
soy sauce, to serve

FOR THE FILLING
200g/7oz block tuna for sashimi
200g/7oz block salmon for sashimi
30ml/2 tbsp wasabi paste
½ cucumber, quartered lengthways and seeds removed

FOR THE RICE
400g/14oz/2 cups Japanese rice, washed and drained for 1 hour
25ml/5 tsp sake or dry white wine

FOR THE MIXED VINEGAR
52.5ml/10½ tsp rice vinegar
15ml/1 tbsp sugar
3ml/⅔ tsp salt

MAKES 12 ROLLS OR 72 SLICES

1 Cook the rice, replacing 25ml/5 tsp of the measured cooking water with the sake or wine. Heat the ingredients for the vinegar, stir well and cool. Add the rice.

2 Cut the *yaki-nori* in half lengthways. Cut the fish into four 1cm/½in sauare stickes, the length of the long side of the *nori*. Use two sticks per *nori* if necessary.

3 Place a sheet of *nori*, shiny side downwards, on a bamboo mat on a chopping board.

4 Divide the rice in half in its bowl. Mark each half into six, making 12 portions in all. Spread one portion of the rice over the *nori* with your fingers, leaving a 1cm/½in space uncovered at the top and bottom of the *nori*.

5 Spread a little wasabi in a horizontal line along the middle of the rice and lay a stick of tuna on this.

6 Holding the mat and the edge of the *nori* nearest to you, roll up the *nori* and rice into a tube with the tuna in the middle. Use the mat as a guide – do not roll it into the food. Roll the rice tightly so that it sticks together and encloses the filling firmly.

7 Carefully roll the sushi off the mat. Make 11 other rolls in the same way, four for each filling ingredient. Do not use wasabi paste with the cucumber. Use a wet knife to cut each roll into six slices and stand them on a platter. Wipe and re-rinse the knife occasionally between cuts to stop the rice sticking. Garnish with *gari* and serve soy sauce with the sushi.

YAKITORI CHICKEN

akitori are Japanese-style chicken kebabs. They are easy to eat and ideal for barbecues or parties.

INGREDIENTS
6 boneless chicken thighs, with skin
bunch of spring onions
seven flavour spice, to serve (optional)

FOR THE YAKITORI SAUCE
150ml/¼ pint/⅔ cup soy sauce
90g/3½ oz/½ cup sugar
25ml/5 tsp sake or dry white wine
15ml/1 tbsp plain flour

SERVES 4

1 To make the sauce, stir the soy sauce, sugar and sake or wine into the flour in a small pan and bring to the boil, stirring. Reduce the heat and simmer for 10 minutes, until the sauce is reduced by one-third. Then set aside.

2 Cut each chicken thigh into six chunks and cut the spring onions into 3cm/1¼in long pieces.

3 Thread the chicken and spring onions alternately on to 12 bamboo skewers. Grill under a medium heat or on the barbecue, brushing generously several times with the sauce. Grill for 5–10 minutes, until the chicken is cooked but still moist.

4 Serve with a little extra *yakitori* sauce, and sprinkle the kebabs with seven flavour spice, if liked.

CHICKEN CAKES WITH TERIYAKI SAUCE

These small chicken cakes, about the size of meatballs, are known in Japanese as *Tsukune*.

INGREDIENTS
400g/14oz minced chicken
1 small egg
60ml/4 tbsp grated onion
7.5ml/1½ tsp sugar
7.5ml/1½ tsp soy sauce
cornflour, for coating
15ml/1 tbsp oil
½ bunch of spring onions, finely
shredded, to garnish

FOR THE TERIYAKI SAUCE
30ml/2 tbsp sake or dry white wine
30ml/2 tbsp sugar
30ml/2 tbsp mirin
30ml/2 tbsp soy sauce

SERVES 4

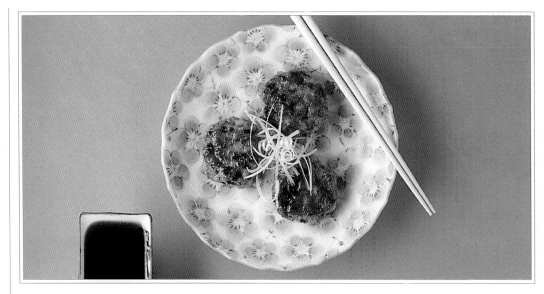

1 Mix the minced chicken with the egg, grated onion, sugar and soy sauce until the ingredients are thoroughly combined and well bound together. This process takes about 3 minutes, until the mixture is quite sticky, which gives a good texture.

2 Shape the mixture into 12 small, flat round cakes and dust them lightly all over with cornflour.

3 Soak the spring onions in a bowl of cold water for 5 minutes and drain well.

4 Heat the oil in a frying pan. Place the chicken cakes in the pan in a single layer, and cook them over a moderate heat for 3 minutes. Turn the cakes over and cook for 3 minutes on the second side.

5 Mix the ingredients for the sauce and pour it into the frying pan. Turn the chicken cakes occasionally until they are evenly glazed with the sauce. Move or gently shake the pan constantly to prevent the sauce from burning.

6 Arrange the chicken cakes on a serving plate and top them with the shredded spring onions. Serve immediately.

SEAFOOD DISHES

Fish and seafood are vital parts of Asian cooking, since many of these countries have extensive coastlines. The freshest seafood is combined with the freshest spices and vegetables, and cooked in the minimum time to preserve the most flavour. Fish and coconut are a favourite combination in Asian cooking, used in curries such as Kashmir Coconut Fish and in peanut sauce for Thai Satay Prawns.

In Chinese dishes the fish is quickly stir-fried with ginger and spring onions, soy sauce and rice wine. Japanese cooking relies on the freshest fish of all, often using raw or lightly marinated tuna, salmon and seafood to make the classic dishes sushi and sashimi.

GRILLED FISH MASALA

These tasty fish fillets with their spicy coating are very simple to prepare. They are cooked using the minimum of oil, so are a healthy option.

INGREDIENTS
4 flat fish fillets, such as plaice, sole or flounder, about 115g/4oz each

FOR THE SPICE MIXTURE
1 garlic clove, crushed
5ml/1 tsp garam masala
5ml/1 tsp chilli powder
1.5ml/¼ tsp ground turmeric
2.5ml/½ tsp salt
15ml/1 tbsp finely chopped fresh coriander
15ml/1 tbsp vegetable oil
30ml/2 tbsp lemon juice
grated carrot, tomato quarters and lime slices, to garnish

SERVES 4

1 Line a flameproof dish or grill pan with foil. Rinse the fish fillets under cold running water, pat dry with kitchen paper and put them into the dish or pan.

2 To make the spice mixture, put the crushed garlic clove and garam masala into a small bowl. Stir in the chilli powder, ground turmeric, the salt and the finely chopped fresh coriander. Gradually add the vegetable oil, stirring constantly. Add the lemon juice and stir thoroughly to mix, then set the spice mixture aside. Preheat the grill to very hot.

3 Lower the temperature of the grill to medium. Using a pastry brush, baste the fish fillets evenly all over with the spice mixture. Grill the fish fillets on each side for about 5 minutes, basting occasionally with the juices that form in the pan, until they are cooked right through.

4 To serve, transfer the fish fillets to a warmed serving platter and make a decorative garnish with the grated carrot, tomato quarters and lime slices. Serve at once, with naan bread, if you like.

COOK'S TIP
For a stronger flavour, brush the fish fillets with the spice mixture an hour or so before you grill them to allow the spices to permeate the flesh.

BALTI FISH IN COCONUT SAUCE

U se fresh fish fillets to make this dish if you can, as they have much more flavour than frozen ones. If you are using frozen fillets, ensure that they are completely thawed before cooking.

INGREDIENTS
30ml/2 tbsp corn oil
5ml/1 tsp onion seeds
4 dried red chillies, crumbled
3 garlic cloves, sliced
1 onion, sliced
2 tomatoes
30ml/2 tbsp desiccated coconut
5ml/1 tsp salt
5ml/1 tsp ground coriander
4 flat fish fillets, such as plaice, sole or flounder, about 75g/3oz each
150ml/¼ pint/⅔ cup water
15ml/1 tbsp lime juice
15ml/1 tbsp chopped fresh coriander
rice or parathas, to serve

SERVES 4

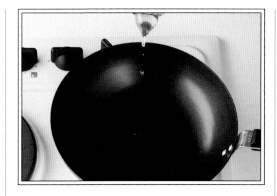

1 Heat the oil in a deep round-bottomed frying pan or a karahi. Lower the heat slightly and add the onion seeds, dried red chillies, garlic and onion. Cook the mixture for 3–4 minutes, stirring once or twice.

2 Cut a cross on the base of each tomato. Plunge the tomatoes into a bowl of boiling water for 20–30 seconds, then into a bowl of cold water. Peel off the skins, then slice thinly. Add the tomatoes, desiccated coconut, salt and ground coriander to the pan and stir to mix thoroughly.

3 Cut each fish fillet into three pieces. Drop the fish pieces into the onion and tomato mixture and turn them gently until they are well coated.

4 Cook for 5–7 minutes, lowering the heat if necessary. Add the measured water, lime juice and chopped fresh coriander and cook for a further 3–5 minutes, until the water has almost all evaporated. Serve the fish with rice or parathas.

COOK'S TIP
Balti is the name of both a deep, rounded frying pan with two ring handles, and the dish cooked in it. Also known as a karahi, the Balti pan is very similar to a wok, which makes an excellent substitute.

KASHMIR COCONUT FISH

F ish and coconut are a popular combination in Asian cooking. This deliciously sweet curry can be served with rice or naan bread.

INGREDIENTS
30ml/2 tbsp vegetable oil
2 onions, sliced
1 green pepper, seeded and sliced
1 garlic clove, crushed
1 dried chilli, seeded and chopped
5ml/1 tsp ground coriander
5ml/1 tsp ground cumin
2.5ml/½ tsp ground turmeric
2.5ml/½ tsp hot chilli powder
2.5ml/½ tsp garam masala
15ml/1 tbsp plain flour
115g/4oz/1⅓ cups creamed coconut
675g/1½lb haddock fillet,
skinned and chopped
4 tomatoes, skinned, seeded and chopped
15ml/1 tbsp lemon juice
30ml/2 tbsp ground almonds
30ml/2 tbsp double cream
salt and freshly ground black pepper
fresh coriander sprigs, to garnish
naan bread and rice, to serve

SERVES 4

1 Heat the oil in a large saucepan and add the onions, pepper and garlic. Cook for 6–7 minutes, until the onions and peppers have softened. Stir in the chopped dried chilli, all the ground spices, the chilli powder, garam masala and flour, and cook for 1 minute.

2 Dissolve the creamed coconut in 600ml/1 pint/2½ cups boiling water and stir into the spicy vegetable mixture. Bring to the boil, cover and then simmer gently for 6 minutes.

3 Add the fish and tomatoes and cook for about 5–6 minutes, or until the fish has turned opaque. Uncover and gently stir in the lemon juice, ground almonds and cream. Season well and garnish with coriander.

COOK'S TIP
You can replace the haddock with other firm-fleshed white fish, such as cod or whiting, or even stir in a few cooked peeled prawns, if liked.

BAKED FISH IN BANANA LEAVES

F ish that is prepared in this way is particularly succulent and flavourful. Fillets are used here rather than whole fish – easier for those who don't like to mess about with bones. It is a great dish for outdoor barbecues.

INGREDIENTS
250ml/8fl oz/1 cup coconut milk
30ml/2 tbsp red curry paste
45ml/3 tbsp fish sauce
30ml/2 tbsp caster sugar
5 kaffir lime leaves, torn
4 × 175g/6oz fish fillets, such
as snapper
175g/6oz mixed vegetables, such as
carrots or leeks, finely shredded
4 banana leaves
30ml/2 tbsp shredded spring onions,
and 2 red chillies, finely sliced,
to garnish

SERVES 4

1 Combine the coconut milk, curry paste, fish sauce, sugar and kaffir lime leaves in a shallow dish.

2 Marinate the fish in this mixture for about 15–30 minutes. Preheat the oven to 200°C/400°F/Gas 6.

3 Mix the vegetables together and lay a portion on top of a banana leaf. Place a piece of fish on top, together with a little of its marinade.

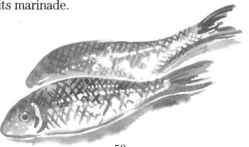

4 Wrap the fish up by turning in the sides and ends of the leaf and secure with cocktail sticks. Repeat with the rest of the leaves and fish.

5 Bake in the hot oven for 20–25 minutes or until the fish is cooked. Alternatively, cook under the grill or on the barbecue. Just before serving, garnish with a sprinkling of spring onions and sliced red chillies.

58

CURRIED PRAWNS IN COCONUT MILK

 curry-like dish from Thailand where the prawns are cooked in a wonderful spicy coconut gravy.

INGREDIENTS
600ml/1 pint/2½ cups coconut milk
30ml/2 tbsp yellow curry paste
(see Cook's Tip)
15ml/1 tbsp fish sauce
2.5ml/½ tsp salt
5ml/1 tsp granulated sugar
450g/1lb king prawns, shelled, tails left
intact and de-veined
225g/8oz cherry tomatoes
juice of ½ lime, to serve
2 red chillies, cut into strips, and
coriander leaves, to garnish

SERVES 4–6

1 Put half the coconut milk into a pan or wok and bring to the boil.

2 Add the yellow curry paste to the coconut milk, stir until it disperses, then simmer for about 10 minutes.

3 Add the fish sauce, salt, sugar and remaining coconut milk. Simmer for another 5 minutes.

4 Add the prawns and cherry tomatoes. Simmer gently for about 5 minutes until the prawns are pink and tender.

5 Serve sprinkled with lime juice and garnished with chillies and coriander.

COOK'S TIP
To make yellow curry paste, process together 6–8 yellow chillies, 1 chopped lemon grass stalk, 4 peeled shallots, 4 garlic cloves, 15ml/1 tbsp peeled chopped root ginger, 5ml/1 tsp coriander seeds, 5ml/1 tsp mustard powder, 5ml/1 tsp salt, 2.5ml/½ tsp ground cinnamon, 15ml/1 tbsp light brown sugar and 30ml/2 tbsp oil in a food processor. When a paste has formed, transfer to a glass jar and chill.

SATAY PRAWNS

n enticing and tasty dish. Lightly cooked greens and jasmine rice make good accompaniments.

INGREDIENTS
450g/1lb king prawns, shelled, tail ends left intact and deveined
½ bunch coriander leaves, 4 red chillies, finely sliced, and spring onions, cut diagonally, to garnish

FOR THE PEANUT SAUCE
45ml/3 tbsp vegetable oil
15ml/1 tbsp chopped garlic
1 small onion, chopped
3–4 red chillies, crushed and chopped
3 kaffir lime leaves, torn
1 lemon grass stalk, bruised and chopped
5ml/1 tsp medium curry paste
250ml/8fl oz/1 cup coconut milk
1.5cm/½in cinnamon stick
75g/3oz crunchy peanut butter
45ml/3 tbsp tamarind juice
30ml/2 tbsp fish sauce
30ml/2 tbsp palm sugar
juice of ½ lemon

SERVES 4–6

1 To make the sauce, heat half the oil in a wok or large frying pan and add the garlic and onion. Cook until it softens, about 3–4 minutes.

2 Add the chillies, kaffir lime leaves, lemon grass and curry paste. Cook for a further 2–3 minutes.

3 Stir in the coconut milk, cinnamon stick, peanut butter, tamarind juice, fish sauce, palm sugar and lemon juice.

4 Reduce the heat and simmer gently for 15–20 minutes until the sauce thickens, stirring occasionally to ensure the sauce doesn't stick to the bottom of the wok or frying pan.

5 Heat the rest of the oil in a wok or large frying pan. Add the prawns and stir-fry for about 3–4 minutes or until the prawns turn pink and are slightly firm to the touch.

6 Mix the prawns with the sauce. Serve garnished with coriander leaves, red chillies and spring onions.

THAI PRAWN SALAD

his salad has the distinctive flavour of lemon grass, an ingredient used widely in South-east Asian cooking.

INGREDIENTS

250g/9oz cooked, peeled
extra large tiger prawns
15ml/1 tbsp fish sauce
30ml/2 tbsp lime juice
2.5ml/½ tsp soft light brown sugar
1 small fresh red chilli, finely chopped
1 spring onion, finely chopped
1 small garlic clove, crushed
2.5cm/1in piece fresh lemon grass,
finely chopped
30ml/2 tbsp chopped fresh coriander
45ml/3 tbsp dry white wine
8–12 lettuce leaves, to serve
fresh coriander sprigs, to garnish

SERVES 4

1 Place the prawns in a bowl and add the fish sauce, lime juice, sugar, chilli, spring onion, garlic and lemon grass. Stir together and then add the coriander and wine. Stir well, cover and leave to marinate in the refrigerator for 2–3 hours until the flavours have permeated the prawns. Mix and turn the prawns from time to time, so that they are evenly coated.

2 Arrange two or three of the lettuce leaves on to four serving plates.

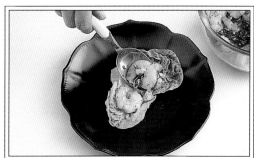

3 Spoon the prawn salad into the lettuce leaves. Garnish with fresh coriander and serve at once.

STIR-FRIED SCALLOPS WITH ASPARAGUS

Asparagus is extremely popular among the Chinese and Thai. The combination of garlic and black pepper gives this dish its spiciness. You can replace the scallops with prawns or other firm variety of seafood.

INGREDIENTS
60ml/4 tbsp vegetable oil
1 bunch asparagus, cut into
5cm/2in lengths
4 garlic cloves, finely chopped
2 shallots, finely chopped
450g/1lb scallops, cleaned
30ml/2 tbsp fish sauce
2.5ml/½ tsp coarsely ground
black pepper
120ml/4fl oz/½ cup coconut milk
coriander leaves, to garnish

SERVES 4–6

1 Heat half the oil in a wok or large frying pan. Add the asparagus and stir-fry for about 2 minutes. Transfer the asparagus to a plate and set aside.

2 Add the rest of the oil, garlic and shallots to the same wok and fry until fragrant. Add the scallops, stir and cook for another 1–2 minutes.

3 Return the asparagus to the wok. Add the fish sauce, ground black pepper and coconut milk.

4 Stir and cook for another 3–4 minutes or until the scallops and asparagus are cooked. Garnish with the coriander leaves.

MALAYSIAN FISH CURRY

T his potent curry, known as *Ikan Moolee*, is often served with Hot Tomato Sambal and plain rice.

INGREDIENTS

*675g/1½ lb monkfish, hokey
or red snapper fillet
45ml/3 tbsp freshly grated
or shredded coconut
30ml/2 tbsp vegetable oil
1 piece* galangal *or fresh ginger,
2.5cm/1in long, peeled and thinly sliced
2 small red chillies, seeded
and finely chopped
2 cloves garlic, crushed
1 piece lemon grass,
5cm/2in long, shredded
1 piece shrimp paste, 1cm/½in square,
or 15ml/1 tbsp fish sauce
400ml/14fl oz/1²⁄₃ cups canned
coconut milk
600ml/1 pint/2½ cups chicken stock
2.5ml/½ tsp turmeric
15ml/1 tbsp sugar
juice of 1 lime or ½ lemon
salt
chunks of lime, freshly chopped
coriander Hot Tomato Sambal, to serve*

SERVES 4–6

1 Cut the fish into large chunks, season with salt and set aside.

2 Dry-fry the coconut in a wok until evenly brown. Add the oil, *galangal* or ginger, chillies, garlic and lemon grass and fry briefly. Stir in the shrimp paste or fish sauce. Strain the coconut milk through a sieve, and add the thin coconut liquid.

3 Add the chicken stock, turmeric, sugar, a little salt and the lime or lemon juice. Simmer for 10 minutes. Add the fish and simmer for a further 6–8 minutes. Stir in the solid coconut milk, simmer gently to thicken. Transfer to a large bowl. Decorate with chunks of lime and coriander to serve.

CHILLI CRABS

 t is possible to find variations on *Kepitang Pedas,* as it's called in Indonesia, all over Asia.

INGREDIENTS
2 cooked crabs, about 675g/1½lb
1cm/½in cube terasi
2 garlic cloves
2 fresh red chillies, seeded, or 5ml/1 tsp
chopped chilli from a jar
2.5cm/1in fresh root ginger,
peeled and sliced
60ml/4 tbsp sunflower oil
300ml/½ pint/1¼ cups tomato ketchup
15ml/1 tbsp dark brown sugar
150ml/¼ pint/⅔ cup warm water
4 spring onions, chopped, to garnish
cucumber chunks and hot toast,
to serve (optional)

SERVES 4

1 Remove the large claws of one crab and turn it on to its back, with the head facing away from you. Push the body up from the main shell. Discard the stomach sac, lungs and any green matter. Leave the brown meat in the shell and cut in half with a cleaver. Cut the body section in half and crack the claws with a sharp blow from a hammer or cleaver. Avoid splintering the claws. Repeat with the other crab.

2 Grind the *terasi,* garlic, chillies and ginger to a paste in a food processor or with a pestle and mortar.

3 Heat a wok or heavy-based pan and add the oil. Fry the spice paste, stirring it all the time, without browning.

4 Stir in the tomato ketchup, sugar and water and mix well. When just boiling, add the crab pieces and toss in the sauce until well coated and hot. Serve in a large bowl, sprinkled with the chopped spring onions. Place in the centre of the table for everyone to help themselves. Accompany with cucumber chunks and hot toast, if using, for mopping up the sauce.

STIR-FRIED SEAFOOD

A colourful and delicious dish from South-east China, combining prawns, squid, and scallops. The squid may be replaced by another fish, or omitted altogether.

INGREDIENTS

115g/4oz squid, cleaned
4–6 fresh scallops
115g/4oz uncooked prawns
½ egg white
15ml/1 tbsp cornflour, mixed with a little water
2–3 celery sticks
1 small red pepper, cored and seeded
2 small carrots
300ml/½ pint/1¼ cups oil
2.5ml/½ tsp finely chopped fresh root ginger
1 spring onion, cut into short sections
5ml/1 tsp salt
2.5ml/½ tsp light brown sugar
15ml/1 tbsp Chinese rice wine or dry sherry
15ml/1 tbsp light soy sauce
5ml/1 tsp hot bean sauce
30ml/2 tbsp chicken stock
few drops of sesame oil, to serve

SERVES 4

1 Open up the squid and, using a sharp knife, score the inside in a criss-cross pattern. Cut the squid into 1cm/½in pieces. Soak the squid in a bowl of boiling water until all the pieces curl up; rinse in cold water and drain.

2 Cut each scallop into 3–4 slices. Peel the prawns and cut each one in half lengthways. In a bowl, mix the scallops and prawns with the egg white and cornflour paste until well blended.

3 Cut the celery, red pepper and carrots into 1–2.5cm/½–1in slices.

4 Heat a wok, then add the oil. When it is medium-hot, add the seafood and stir-fry for about 30–40 seconds. Remove with a large slotted spoon and drain.

5 Pour off the excess oil, leaving about 30ml/2 tbsp in the wok, and add the vegetables with the ginger and spring onion. Stir-fry for about 1 minute.

6 Return the seafood to the wok, stir for another 30–40 seconds, then stir in the salt, sugar, wine or sherry, soy sauce and hot bean sauce. Add the stock and stir for about 1 minute. Serve sprinkled with sesame oil.

PRAWN FU-YUNG

This is a very colourful dish that is simple to make. Most of the preparation can be done well in advance. It comes from the south of China.

INGREDIENTS
3 eggs, beaten, reserving 5ml/1 tsp of egg white
5ml/1 tsp salt
15ml/1 tbsp finely chopped spring onions
45–60ml/3–4 tbsp vegetable oil
225g/8oz uncooked prawns, peeled
10ml/2 tsp cornflour, mixed with a little water
175g/6oz peas
15ml/1 tbsp Chinese rice wine or dry sherry

SERVES 4

1 Beat the eggs with a pinch of the salt, and a little of the spring onion. In a wok, scramble the eggs in a little oil over a moderate heat. Remove and reserve.

2 Mix the prawns with a little of the salt, the egg white, and cornflour paste. Heat the oil in a wok. When it is hot, add the peas and stir-fry for 30 seconds. Add the prawns.

3 Add the spring onions, and stir-fry for 1 further minute, then stir the mixture into the scrambled egg with the last of the salt and the wine or sherry. Blend well and serve immediately.

BRAISED FISH WITH MUSHROOMS

T his is a Chinese version of the French *filets de sole bonne femme* (sole with mushrooms and wine sauce), with oriental flavours.

INGREDIENTS

450g/1lb fillets of lemon sole or plaice
½ egg white
30ml/2 tbsp cornflour, mixed with a little water
600ml/1 pint/2½ cups vegetable oil
15ml/1 tbsp finely chopped spring onions
2.5ml/½ tsp finely chopped fresh root ginger
115g/4oz white mushrooms, thinly sliced
5ml/1 tsp light brown sugar
15ml/1 tbsp light soy sauce
30ml/2 tbsp Chinese rice wine or dry sherry
15ml/1 tbsp brandy
120ml/4fl oz/½ cup chicken stock
salt
few drops of sesame oil, to serve

SERVES 4

1 Trim off the soft bones along the edge of the fish, but leave the skin on. Cut each fillet into bite-size pieces. Put a little salt, the egg white and about half of the cornflour paste into a small bowl and mix together. Coat the fish pieces in the mixture.

2 Heat the oil in a wok until medium-hot, add the fish pieces one at a time and stir gently so they do not stick. Remove after about 1 minute and drain. Pour off all but 30ml/2 tbsp of oil. Stir-fry the spring onions, ginger and mushrooms for 1 minute.

3 Add the sugar, light soy sauce, rice wine or sherry, the brandy and stock and bring to the boil. Add the fish pieces and braise for 1 minute. Thicken with the remaining cornflour paste and sprinkle with sesame oil. Serve immediately.

FIVE-SPICE FISH

C hinese mixtures of spicy, sweet and sour flavours are particularly successful with fish, and dinner is ready in minutes.

INGREDIENTS

4 white fish fillets, such as cod, haddock
or flounder, about 175g/6oz each
5ml/1 tsp five-spice powder
20ml/4 tsp cornflour
15ml/1 tbsp sesame or sunflower oil
3 spring onions, finely sliced
5ml/1 tsp finely chopped fresh root ginger
150g/5oz button mushrooms, sliced
115g/4oz baby sweetcorn, sliced
30ml/2 tbsp soy sauce
45ml/3 tbsp dry sherry or apple juice
5ml/1 tsp sugar
salt and ground black pepper
stir-fried vegetables, to serve

SERVES 4

1 Toss the fish fillets in the five-spice powder and cornflour to coat.

2 Heat the oil in a wok or frying pan and stir-fry the spring onions, ginger, mushrooms and sweetcorn for about 1 minute. Add the fish fillets and cook for 2–3 minutes, turning once.

3 In a small bowl, mix together the soy sauce, sherry or juice and sugar, then pour over the fish. Simmer for 2 minutes, season, then serve immediately with stir-fried vegetables.

STEAMED FISH WITH GINGER

Any firm-fleshed fish with a delicate taste, such as salmon or turbot, can be cooked by this method. The sweet taste of ginger combined with spring onions makes this dish a firm favourite on mainland China.

INGREDIENTS

1 sea bass, trout or striped mullet,
weighing about 675g/1½lb, cleaned
2.5ml/½ tsp salt
15ml/1 tbsp sesame oil
2–3 spring onions, cut in half lengthways
30ml/2 tbsp light soy sauce
30ml/2 tbsp Chinese rice wine or
dry sherry
15ml/1 tbsp finely grated fresh root ginger
30ml/2 tbsp vegetable oil
finely shredded spring onions, to garnish

SERVES 4–6

1 Using a sharp knife, score both sides of the fish as far down as the bone, making several diagonal cuts about 2.5cm/1in apart. Rub the fish all over, inside and out, with salt and sesame oil.

2 Scatter the spring onions evenly over a heatproof platter and place the fish on top. Blend the soy sauce and wine or sherry with the ginger and pour over the fish.

3 Place the platter in a steamer over boiling water (or inside a wok on a rack), and steam vigorously, covered, for about 12–15 minutes until the fish is cooked *(left)*.

4 Heat the oil in a small saucepan; remove the platter from the steamer, place the shredded spring onions on top of the fish, then pour the hot oil along the whole length of the fish. Serve immediately.

RED AND WHITE PRAWNS

T he Chinese name for this dish is Yuan Yang Prawns. Pairs of mandarin ducks are also known as *Yuan Yang,* or love birds, because they are always seen together. They symbolize affection and happiness.

INGREDIENTS
450g/1lb uncooked prawns
pinch of salt
½ egg white
15ml/1 tbsp cornflour, mixed with a little water
175g/6oz mange-touts
600ml/1 pint/2½ cups vegetable oil
2.5ml/½ tsp salt
5ml/1 tsp light brown sugar
15ml/1 tbsp finely chopped spring onions
5ml/1 tsp finely chopped fresh root ginger
15ml/1 tbsp light soy sauce
15ml/1 tbsp Chinese rice wine or dry sherry
5ml/1 tsp hot bean sauce
15ml/1 tbsp tomato purée

SERVES 4–6

1 Peel and de-vein the prawns, and mix with the salt, egg white and cornflour paste. Top and tail the mange-touts.

2 Heat a wok, then add 30–45ml/ 2–3 tbsp of the oil. When it is hot, add the mange-touts and stir-fry for about 1 minute, then add the salt and sugar and continue stirring for 1 further minute. Remove the mange-touts with a slotted spoon and place in the centre of a warmed serving platter.

3 Heat the remaining oil, partially cook the prawns for 1 minute, remove, and drain on kitchen paper.

4 Pour off the excess oil, leaving about 15ml/1 tbsp in the wok, and add the spring onions, ginger and prawns. Stir-fry for 1 minute, then add the soy sauce and wine or sherry. Blend well and place half of the prawns at one end of the platter.

5 Add the hot bean sauce and tomato purée to the remaining prawns. Blend well and place the "red" prawns at the other end of the platter. Serve at once.

TUNA RICE BOWL

ne of the most popular dishes in Japan, *Tekka-don* consists of rice with fresh tuna laid on top.

INGREDIENTS

480g/1lb 1oz/2¼ cups Japanese rice, washed and drained for 1 hour
30ml/2 tbsp sake or dry white wine
300g/11oz block tuna for sashimi
1 sheet yaki-nori *seaweed*
lettuce and 20ml/4 tsp wasabi paste, to garnish
soy sauce, to serve

SERVES 4

1 Cook the rice, replacing 30ml/2 tbsp of the measured cooking water with the sake or wine.

2 Cut thin slices of tuna, tilting it to the side. Cut towards you from the far side.

3 Using scissors, cut the *yaki-nori* seaweed very carefully into 5cm/2in size pieces in length.

4 The rice must be at room temperature, so as not to cook the tuna. Divide it among four bowls.

5 Arrange the tuna on top of the rice and sprinkle the seaweed gently over the top. Garnish with lettuce and 5ml/1 tsp of the wasabi paste for each plate, and serve immediately with soy sauce.

SLICED RAW SALMON

Sliced fresh fish is known as sashimi in Japan. This recipe introduces the cutting technique known as *hira zukuri*. Salmon is a good choice for those who have not tried sashimi before because most people are familiar with smoked salmon which is also uncooked.

INGREDIENTS
2 fresh salmon fillets, skinned and any bones removed, about 400g/14oz total weight
soy sauce, to serve

FOR THE GARNISH
50g/2oz/¼ cup mooli
20ml/4 tsp wasabi paste
shiso leaf

SERVES 4

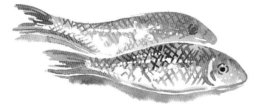

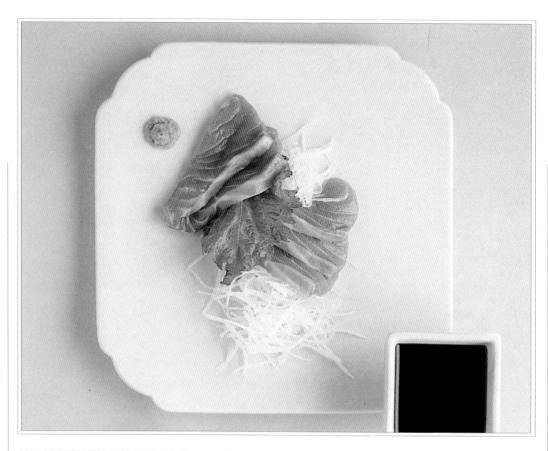

1 Put the salmon fillets in a freezer for about 10 minutes to make them easier to cut, then lay them skinned side up with the thick end to your right and away from you. Tilt the fish to the left.

2 Slice the fish towards you, starting the cut from the point of the knife, then slide the slice away from the fillet, to the right. Always slice from the far side towards you.

3 Using a sharp knife, finely shred the mooli. Place it in a large bowl of cold water and leave it for about 5 minutes, then drain it well.

4 Place three slices of prepared salmon on a serving plate, then overlap another two slices on them diagonally. You can arrange fewer or more slices per portion, but an odd number looks better.

5 Garnish each plate of salmon with the finely shredded mooli, wasabi paste and a shiso leaf, then serve the dish immediately with a small bowl of soy sauce as an accompaniment to dip into.

SHAPED SUSHI

 his exciting and fresh sushi dish includes some sashimi, which are slices of raw fish.

INGREDIENTS
480g/1lb 1oz/2¼ cups Japanese rice, washed and drained for 1 hour
30ml/2 tbsp sake or dry white wine
1 Rolled Omelette
5ml/1 tsp wasabi paste
soy sauce, gari and lettuce, to serve

FOR THE SUSHI VINEGAR
60ml/4 tbsp rice vinegar
15ml/1 tbsp sugar
5ml/1 tsp salt

FOR THE SEAFOOD GARNISH
1 squid body sack, skinned, about 200g/7oz total weight
1 leg boiled octopus
200g/7oz block tuna for sashimi
200g/7oz block salmon for sashimi
4 raw prawns with shells, heads removed

FOR THE MARINADE
15ml/1 tbsp rice vinegar
5ml/1 tsp sugar
pinch of salt

SERVES 4

1 Cook the rice, replacing 30ml/2 tbsp of the measured cooking water with the sake or wine.

2 Meanwhile, heat the ingredients for the sushi vinegar, stir well and cool. Add this to the hot cooked rice, stir well with a spatula, at the same time fanning the rice constantly – this gives the rice an attractive glaze. Cover with a damp dish cloth and leave to cool. Do not put in the fridge, as this will make the rice go hard.

3 Cut the squid into strips measuring 2–3cm/¾–1¼in wide and 5cm/2in long. Carefully, slice the octopus leg into strips of the same size. Cut the block tuna and salmon into pieces of similar size, about 3mm/⅛in thick.

4 Thread the prawns on bamboo skewers from tail to head to make sure they lie flat when cooked. Boil for 1 minute, then remove the skewers and shells, leaving the tails intact. Slit each prawn along the belly, taking care not to cut through, and remove the dark vein. Open each one up like a book.

5 Mix the marinade ingredients in a dish, add the prawns and leave aside for about 10 minutes.

6 Slice the Rolled Omelette into 5mm/¼in thick pieces.

7 Wet your hands with some cold water, and then carefully shape about 15–20g/½–¾oz rice into a rectangle measuring 1cm/½in high, 2cm/¾in wide and 5cm/2in long. Repeat this process with the remaining rice.

8 Use your finger to spread a little wasabi paste on to the middle of each rice rectangle and divide the seafood among the rectangles, laying them on top. Do not add wasabi paste for egg sushi.

9 Serve the sushi immediately, with soy sauce, *gari* and lettuce. The *gari* may be eaten to cleanse the palate after each mouthful, if liked.

SALMON SEALED WITH EGG

Tamago-toji, meaning egg cover, is the Japanese title for this type of dish which can be made from various ingredients. Canned pink salmon is used here for a very delicate flavour. Fried tofu can be used instead of salmon.

INGREDIENTS
400g/14oz can pink salmon, drained,
bones and skin removed
10 mangetouts, trimmed
2 large mild onions, sliced
40ml/8 tsp sugar
30ml/2 tbsp soy sauce
4 small eggs, beaten

SERVES 4

1 Flake the canned salmon. Boil the trimmed mangetouts for 2–3 minutes, drain and slice finely.

2 Put the sliced onions in a frying pan, add 200ml/7fl oz/scant 1 cup water and bring to the boil. Cook for 5 minutes over a moderate heat, then add the sugar and soy sauce. Cook for a further 5 minutes.

3 Add the flaked salmon and cook for 2–3 minutes, or until the soup has virtually evaporated. Pour the egg over to cover the surface. Sprinkle in the mangetouts and cover the pan. Cook for 1 minute over a moderate heat, until just set. Do not overcook or the eggs will curdle and separate. Spoon on to a plate from the pan and serve immediately.

FRIED SWORDFISH

This is a light and tasty cold dish that is suitable for serving on a hot summer's day. Dashi is a stock that provides the underlying flavour for most Japanese dishes.

INGREDIENTS
4 swordfish steaks, boned, skin left on,
about 600g/1lb 5oz total weight
15ml/1 tbsp soy sauce
7.5ml/1½ tsp rice vinegar
bunch of spring onions
4 asparagus spears, trimmed
30ml/2 tbsp oil

FOR THE MARINADE
45ml/3 tbsp soy sauce
45ml/3 tbsp rice vinegar
30ml/2 tbsp sake or dry white wine
15ml/1 tbsp sugar
15ml/1 tbsp instant dashi or water
7.5ml/1½ tsp sesame oil

SERVES 4

1 Cut the swordfish steaks into 4cm/1½in chunks and place in a dish. Pour the 15ml/1 tbsp soy sauce and 7.5ml/1½ tsp rice vinegar over the fish, then set aside for about 5 minutes. Meanwhile, cut the spring onions into 3cm/1¼in lengths and the asparagus spears into 4cm/1½in lengths.

2 Mix the ingredients for the marinade in a dish. Heat three-quarters of the oil in a frying pan. Wipe the swordfish with kitchen paper and fry over a moderate heat for about 1–2 minutes on each side, or until cooked. Remove the fish from the frying pan and place it in the marinade.

3 Clean the frying pan and heat the remaining oil in it. Fry the spring onions over a moderate heat until browned, then add them to the fish. Fry the asparagus in the oil remaining in the pan over a low heat for 3–4 minutes, then add to the fish.

4 Leave the fish and vegetables to marinate for 10–20 minutes, turning the pieces occasionally. Serve the cold fish with the marinade on a large, deep plate.

POACHED MACKEREL WITH MISO

This dish, *Mackerel Miso-ni*, is typical of Japanese-style home cooking. There are many types of Japanese miso bean paste, including white miso which is sweet in flavour and dark miso which tastes salty. Darker miso is preferred for this recipe, but you can use any type.

INGREDIENTS

1 mackerel, gutted, 675–750g/1½ –1¾lb
300ml/½ pint/1¼ cups instant dashi
30ml/2 tbsp sugar
60ml/4 tbsp sake or dry white wine
10g/¼oz fresh root ginger, peeled and finely sliced
115g/4oz/½ cup miso
10g/¼oz fresh root ginger, peeled and finely shredded, to garnish

SERVES 4

COOK'S TIP
When boiling fish, gently lower it into boiling water. Do not cook it from cold, as the fish will smell unpleasant and the cooking liquid or soup will taste bitter.

1 Chop the head off the mackerel and cut the fish into 2cm/¾in thick steaks. Soak the shredded ginger for the garnish in cold water for 5 minutes, then drain well.

2 Fold a sheet of foil just smaller than the diameter of a large shallow pan. Pour the dashi, sugar and sake or wine into the pan. Bring to the boil, then arrange the mackerel in the pan in a single layer and add the sliced ginger. Spoon the soup over the mackerel, then place the foil over it. Simmer the mackerel for 5–6 minutes.

3 Dissolve the miso in a small mixing bowl in a little of the soup liquid from the saucepan. Carefully pour it back into the saucepan and simmer it for 12 minutes more, spooning the soup over the mackerel occasionally as it cooks.

4 Use a slotted spoon to remove the mackerel carefully from the saucepan and place it on a serving plate. Spoon the remaining soup over the top and garnish the dish with the finely shredded ginger. Serve the mackerel hot.

TERIYAKI TROUT

Teriyaki sauce is very useful, not only for fish but also for meat. It is a delicious sweet soy-based sauce that creates a lovely shiny gloss which is very attractive.

INGREDIENTS
4 trout fillets

FOR THE TERIYAKI MARINADE
75ml/5 tbsp soy sauce
75ml/5 tbsp sake or dry white wine
75ml/5 tbsp mirin

SERVES 4

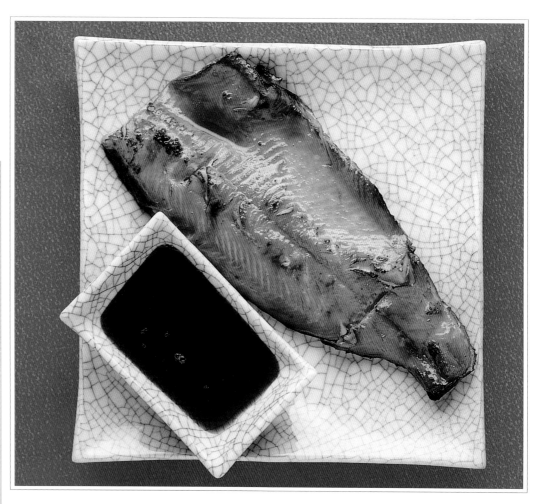

1 Lay the fillets in a shallow dish in a single layer. Mix the marinade ingredients and pour over the fish. Cover and marinate in the fridge for 5–6 hours. Turn occasionally.

2 Thread two trout fillets neatly together on two metal skewers. Repeat with the remaining two fillets. You could cut the fillets in half if they are too big.

3 Grill the trout fillets on a barbecue over a high heat. Be sure to keep the fish about 10cm/4in away from the flame and brush it with the marinade several times during cooking. Grill each side of the fish until shiny and the trout is cooked through. Alternatively, cook the trout under a conventional grill.

4 Slide the trout off the metal skewers while it is still hot. Serve the fillets either hot or cold with any remaining marinade poured over the top.

POULTRY DISHES

Chicken lends itself perfectly to stir-frying, one of the most popular forms of Asian cooking. The Chinese use a wok to stir-fry their dishes, cutting both meat and vegetables into small pieces and cooking them at high temperatures to retain their flavour and vitamins.

Balti cooking uses a karahi, an Indian version of the wok, to make delicious combinations of poultry, vegetables and spices. Try Poussins in Tamarind Sauce for an unusual combination of sweet, sour and spicy flavours. Chicken salad may not sound like an Asian dish but this section includes three delicious varieties. Tangy Chicken Salad, Chiang Mai Salad and Hot and Sour Chicken Salad, all three from Vietnam and Thailand, elevate this humble dish to something very special.

KHARA MASALA CHICKEN

W hole spices (*khara*) are used in this recipe, giving it a wonderfully rich flavour. This is a dry dish so it is best served with a raita and Parathas.

INGREDIENTS

1.5ml/¼ tsp mustard seeds
1.5ml/¼ tsp each fennel and onion seeds
2 curry leaves
2.5ml/½ tsp crushed dried red chillies
2.5ml/½ tsp white cumin seeds
1.5ml/¼ tsp fenugreek seeds
2.5ml/½ tsp crushed pomegranate seeds
5ml/1 tsp salt
5ml/1 tsp sliced fresh root ginger
3 garlic cloves, sliced
60ml/4 tbsp corn oil
4 large fresh green chillies, slit
1 large onion, sliced
1 tomato, sliced
675g/1½lb chicken, skinned, boned and cubed
chopped fresh coriander, to garnish

SERVES 4

1 Mix together the mustard, fennel and onion seeds, curry leaves, crushed red chillies, cumin seeds, fenugreek seeds, crushed pomegranate seeds and salt in a large bowl, then add the ginger and garlic.

2 Heat the oil in a medium karahi or deep round-bottomed frying pan and stir in the spice mixture and green chillies. Add the onion and cook over a moderate heat, stirring occasionally for 5–7 minutes until the onion is soft and translucent.

3 Add the tomato and chicken pieces to the karahi and cook over a moderate heat for about 7 minutes, or until the chicken is cooked through and the sauce has thickened and reduced.

4 Stir the tomato and chicken mixture together thoroughly and continue cooking over a gentle heat for a further 3–5 minutes, until most of the sauce has reduced. Garnish the chicken with chopped fresh coriander and serve immediately.

CHILLI CHICKEN

Hot and spicy is the best way of describing this Balti dish. The aroma of the fresh chillies cooking is truly mouth-watering!

INGREDIENTS
75ml/5 tbsp corn oil
8 large fresh green chillies, slit
2.5ml/½ tsp mixed onion and
cumin seeds
4 curry leaves
5ml/1 tsp sliced fresh root ginger
5ml/1 tsp chilli powder
5ml/1 tsp ground coriander
1 garlic clove, crushed
5ml/1 tsp salt
2 onions, chopped
675g/1½lb chicken, skinned, boned
and cubed
15ml/1 tbsp lemon juice
15ml/1 tbsp roughly chopped fresh mint
15ml/1 tbsp roughly chopped
fresh coriander
8–10 cherry tomatoes

SERVES 4–6

1 Heat the oil in a deep round-bottomed frying pan or a karahi. Lower the heat slightly, add the slit green chillies and fry until the skins start to change colour. Remove the chillies to a plate.

2 Add the onion and cumin seeds, curry leaves, ginger, chilli powder, ground coriander, garlic, salt and onions to the pan and fry for a few seconds, stirring the mixture constantly.

3 Add the chicken pieces and stir-fry for 7–10 minutes, or until the chicken is cooked right through.

4 Sprinkle the lemon juice over the chicken and add the mint and coriander.

5 Add the cherry tomatoes and return the chillies to the pan. Heat through and serve with Naan Bread or Parathas.

CHICKEN PASANDA

asanda dishes are firm favourites in Pakistan and now they are becoming so in the West.

INGREDIENTS

60ml/4 tbsp Greek yogurt
2.5ml/½ tsp black cumin seeds
4 cardamom pods
6 whole black peppercorns
10ml/2 tsp garam masala
2.5cm/1in piece cinnamon stick
15ml/1 tbsp ground almonds
1 garlic clove, crushed
5ml/1 tsp sliced fresh root ginger
5ml/1 tsp chilli powder
5ml/1 tsp salt
675g/1½lb chicken, skinned, boned and cubed
75ml/5 tbsp corn oil
2 onions, diced
3 fresh green chillies, chopped
30ml/2 tbsp chopped fresh coriander
120ml/4fl oz/½ cup single cream

SERVES 4

1 Mix the yogurt, cumin seeds, cardamom pods, peppercorns, garam masala, cinnamon stick, ground almonds, garlic, ginger, chilli powder and salt in a medium bowl. Add the chicken pieces, cover and leave to marinate for about 2 hours.

2 Heat the oil in a large karahi or deep round-bottomed frying pan. Add the onions and fry for 2–3 minutes.

3 Add the chicken mixture and stir until it is thoroughly combined with the onions.

4 Cook the chicken and spice mixture over a moderate heat, stirring occasionally, for 12–15 minutes, or until the sauce is thickened and the chicken pieces are cooked through.

5 Add the green chillies and fresh coriander, pour in the cream and bring to the boil. Serve garnished with more coriander, if wished.

BALTI CHICKEN WITH LENTILS

This recipe has a rather unusual combination of flavours, but it is well worth trying. The mango powder gives a delicious tangy flavour to the finished dish.

INGREDIENTS

75g/3oz/½ cup chana dhal (split yellow lentils)
60ml/4 tbsp corn oil
2 leeks, chopped
6 dried red chillies
4 curry leaves
5ml/1 tsp mustard seeds
10ml/2 tsp mango powder
2 tomatoes, chopped
2.5ml/½ tsp chilli powder
5ml/1 tsp ground coriander
5ml/1 tsp salt
450g/1lb chicken, skinned, boned and cubed
15ml/1 tbsp chopped fresh coriander

SERVES 4–6

COOK'S TIP
Chana dhal is available from Asian stores. However, split yellow peas from delicatessens and supermarkets make a good substitute.

1 Wash the lentils carefully under cold running water and remove any stones or pieces of grit.

2 Put the lentils into a saucepan with enough water to cover and boil for about 10 minutes until they are soft but not mushy. Drain and set aside in a bowl.

3 Heat the oil in a medium karahi or deep round-bottomed frying pan. Lower the heat slightly and add the leeks, dried red chillies, curry leaves and mustard seeds. Stir-fry gently for a few minutes.

4 Add the mango powder, tomatoes, chilli powder, ground coriander, salt and chicken and stir-fry for 7–10 minutes.

5 Mix in the cooked lentils and fry for a further 2 minutes, or until the chicken is thoroughly cooked.

6 Garnish with the fresh coriander and serve at once.

BALTI POUSSINS IN TAMARIND SAUCE

The chillies make this a quite hot Balti dish. Its subtle, sweet and sour flavour is due to the addition of the tamarind paste.

INGREDIENTS

60ml/4 tbsp tomato ketchup
15ml/1 tbsp tamarind paste
60ml/4 tbsp water
7.5ml/1½ tsp chilli powder
7.5ml/1½ tsp salt
15ml/1 tbsp sugar
7.5ml/1½ tsp sliced fresh root ginger
1½ garlic cloves, crushed
30ml/2 tbsp desiccated coconut
30ml/2 tbsp sesame seeds
5ml/1 tsp poppy seeds
5ml/1 tsp ground cumin
7.5ml/1½ tsp ground coriander
2 × 450g/1lb poussins, skinned and cut into 6–8 pieces each
75ml/5 tbsp corn oil
8 curry leaves
2.5ml/½ tsp onion seeds
3 large dried red chillies
2.5ml/½ tsp fenugreek seeds
10–12 cherry tomatoes
45ml/3 tbsp chopped fresh coriander
2 fresh green chillies, chopped

SERVES 4–6

1 Put the tomato ketchup, tamarind paste and water into a large bowl and blend together with a fork until they are thoroughly combined.

2 Add the chilli powder, salt, sugar, ginger, garlic, coconut, sesame and poppy seeds, ground cumin and ground coriander to the mixture.

3 Add the poussin pieces and stir until they are well coated with the spice mixture. Set aside.

4 Heat the oil in a deep round-bottomed frying pan or a large karahi. Add the curry leaves, onion seeds, red chillies and fenugreek seeds and fry for 1 minute.

5 Lower the heat to moderate and add the poussin pieces with their sauce and stir well. Simmer for about 12–15 minutes, or until the poussin is thoroughly cooked.

6 Add the tomatoes, fresh coriander and green chillies, and serve with Colourful Pullao Rice if wished.

CHICKEN BIRYANI

This is a classic Indian dish for important occasions, and is truly fit for royalty. Serve it on a wide, shallow platter for maximum effect.

INGREDIENTS
1.5kg/3–3½lb skinless, boneless chicken breast, cut into large pieces
60ml/4 tbsp biryani masala paste
2 green chillies, chopped
15ml/1 tbsp grated fresh root ginger
2 garlic cloves, crushed
50g/2oz fresh coriander, chopped
6–8 fresh mint leaves, chopped
150ml/¼ pint/⅔ cup natural yogurt
4 onions, sliced, deep-fried and crushed
450g/1lb/2½ cups basmati rice, washed
5ml/1 tsp black cumin seeds
5cm/2in cinnamon stick
6 green cardamom pods
vegetable oil, for shallow frying
4 large potatoes, peeled and quartered
300ml/½ pint/1¼ cups skimmed milk
few saffron strands, infused in milk
salt
30ml/2 tbsp ghee or unsalted butter, plus extra for shallow-frying,
50g/2oz/½ cup cashew nuts and
50g/2oz/⅓ cup sultanas, to garnish

Serves 4–6

1 Mix the chicken with the next nine ingredients in a large bowl, cover and leave to marinate for about 2 hours. Place in a large heavy pan and cook gently for about 10 minutes. Set aside.

2 Boil a large pan of water. Add the rice with the cumin seeds, cinnamon stick and cardamom pods; soak for 5 minutes. Drain well. Remove the whole spices.

3 Heat the oil for shallow-frying and fry the potatoes until they are evenly browned on all sides. Drain and set aside.

4 Arrange half of the rice on top of the chicken pieces in the saucepan in an even layer, then make another even layer with the potatoes. Put the remaining rice on top of the potatoes and spread it out to make an even layer.

5 Sprinkle the skimmed milk all over the rice. Make random holes through the rice with the handle of a spoon and pour a little saffron-flavoured milk into each one. Place a few knobs of ghee or butter on the surface of the rice, cover the pan tightly and cook over a low heat for 35–45 minutes.

6 While the biryani is cooking, make the garnish. Heat a little ghee or butter and fry the cashew nuts and sultanas until they swell. Drain and set aside. When the biryani is ready, gently toss the rice, chicken and potatoes together. Transfer to a warmed serving platter, garnish with the nut and sultana mixture and serve immediately.

CHICKEN IN A CASHEW NUT SAUCE

This chicken dish has a deliciously thick and nutty sauce, and is best served with plain boiled rice. Cashew nuts grow profusely in southern India and are widely used in cooking.

INGREDIENTS

2 onions

30ml/2 tbsp tomato purée

50g/2oz/½ cup cashew nuts

7.5ml/1½ tsp garam masala

1 garlic clove, crushed

5ml/1 tsp chilli powder

15ml/1 tbsp lemon juice

1.5ml/¼ tsp ground turmeric

5ml/1 tsp salt

15ml/1 tbsp natural yogurt

30ml/2 tbsp corn oil

15ml/1 tbsp chopped fresh coriander

15ml/1 tbsp sultanas

450g/1lb skinless, boneless chicken breasts, cut into pieces

175g/6oz button mushrooms

300ml/½ pint/1¼ cups water

15ml/1 tbsp chopped fresh coriander, to garnish

SERVES 4

1 Cut the onions into quarters and place in a food processor or blender. Process for about 1 minute.

2 Add the tomato purée, cashew nuts, garam masala, garlic, chilli powder, lemon juice, turmeric, salt and yogurt and process for a further 1–1½ minutes.

3 Heat the oil in a saucepan and pour in the spice mixture. Fry for 2 minutes, over a medium to low heat. Add the coriander, sultanas and chicken, and stir-fry the mixture for 1 minute.

4 Add the mushrooms, pour in the water and bring to a simmer. Cover the saucepan and cook over a low heat for about 10 minutes. Check that the chicken is cooked through and the sauce is thick. Cook for a little longer, if necessary.

5 To serve, ladle the chicken and its sauce on to a warmed serving dish. Garnish with the chopped coriander.

BARBECUED CHICKEN

Barbecued chicken is served almost everywhere in Thailand, from portable roadside stalls to sports stadiums and beaches. For an authentic touch, serve with rice on a banana leaf.

INGREDIENTS
1 chicken, about 1.5kg/3–3½ lb,
cut into 8–10 pieces
2 limes, cut into wedges,
2 red chillies, finely sliced, and
a few lemon grass stalks, to garnish

FOR THE MARINADE
2 lemon grass stalks, chopped
2.5cm/1in piece fresh root ginger
6 garlic cloves
4 shallots
½ bunch coriander roots
15ml/1 tbsp palm sugar
120ml/4fl oz/½ cup coconut milk
30ml/2 tbsp fish sauce
30ml/2 tbsp soy sauce

SERVES 4–6

1 To make the marinade, put all the ingredients into a food processor and process until smooth.

2 Put the chicken pieces in a dish and pour over the marinade. Leave in a cool place to marinate for at least 4 hours, or preferably overnight.

3 Barbecue the chicken over glowing coals, or place it on a rack over a baking tray and bake at 200°C/400°F/Gas 6 for about 20–30 minutes or until the chicken is cooked and golden brown. Turn the pieces occasionally and brush with the marinade.

4 Garnish with lime wedges, finely sliced red chillies and lemon grass.

STIR-FRIED CHICKEN WITH BASIL AND CHILLIES

This quick and easy chicken dish is an excellent introduction to Thai cuisine. Deep frying the basil adds another dimension to this recipe. Thai basil, also known as holy basil, has a unique, pungent flavour that is both spicy and sharp. The dull leaves have serrated edges.

INGREDIENTS
45ml/3 tbsp vegetable oil
4 garlic cloves, sliced
2–4 red chillies, seeded and chopped
450g/1lb chicken, cut into bite-size pieces
30–45ml/2–3 tbsp fish sauce
10ml/2 tsp dark soy sauce
5ml/1 tsp sugar
10–12 Thai basil leaves
2 red chillies, finely sliced, and 20 Thai basil leaves, deep fried (optional), to garnish

SERVES 4–6

COOK'S TIP
To deep fry Thai basil leaves, make sure that the leaves are completely dry. Deep fry in hot oil for about 30–40 seconds, lift out and drain on kitchen paper.

1 Heat the oil in a wok or large frying pan and swirl it around.

2 Add the garlic and chillies and stir-fry until golden.

3 Add the chicken and stir-fry until it changes colour.

4 Season with fish sauce, soy sauce and sugar. Continue to stir-fry for another 3–4 minutes or until the chicken is cooked through. Stir in the fresh Thai basil leaves. Garnish with sliced red chillies and the deep fried basil, if using.

RED CHICKEN CURRY WITH BAMBOO SHOOTS

amboo shoots lend a crunchy texture to this classic Thai dish.

INGREDIENTS
1 litre/1¾ pints/4 cups coconut milk
450g/1lb diced boneless chicken
30ml/2 tbsp fish sauce
15ml/1 tbsp granulated sugar
225g/8oz bamboo shoots, sliced
5 kaffir lime leaves, torn
salt and freshly ground black pepper
chillies, basil and mint leaves, to garnish

FOR THE RED CURRY PASTE
12–15 red chillies, seeded
4 shallots, thinly sliced
2 garlic cloves, chopped
15ml/1 tbsp chopped galangal
2 stalks lemon grass, chopped
3 kaffir lime leaves, chopped
4 coriander roots
10 black peppercorns
5ml/1 tsp coriander seeds
2.5ml/½ tsp cumin seeds
good pinch of ground cinnamon
5ml/1 tsp ground turmeric
2.5ml/½ tsp shrimp paste
5ml/1 tsp salt
30ml/2 tbsp oil

SERVES 4–6

1 *For the red curry paste, combine the all the ingredients in a pestle and mortar except for the oil, and pound until smooth.*

2 *Add the oil a little at a time and blend in well. Place in a jar in the*

3 In a large heavy-based saucepan, bring half the coconut milk to the boil, stirring until it separates.

4 Add 30ml/2 tbsp red curry paste and cook for a few minutes.

5 Add the chicken, fish sauce and sugar. Fry for 3–5 minutes until the chicken changes colour, stirring constantly to prevent it from sticking to the pan.

6 Add the rest of the coconut milk, bamboo shoots and lime leaves. Return to the boil. Season to taste. Serve garnished with chillies, basil and mint leaves.

COOK'S TIP
It is quite acceptable to use canned bamboo, if fresh bamboo is not available. Whenever possible, buy whole canned bamboo, as it is generally crisper and of better quality than sliced shoots.

TANGY CHICKEN SALAD

his fresh and lively dish typifies the character of Thai cuisine. It is ideal for a starter or light lunch.

INGREDIENTS
4 skinned, boneless chicken breasts
2 garlic cloves, crushed and roughly chopped
30ml/2 tbsp soy sauce
30ml/2 tbsp vegetable oil
120ml/4fl oz/½ cup coconut cream
30ml/2 tbsp fish sauce
juice of 1 lime
30ml/2 tbsp palm sugar
115g/4oz water chestnuts, sliced
50g/2oz cashew nuts, roasted
4 shallots, finely sliced
4 kaffir lime leaves, finely sliced
1 lemon grass stalk, finely sliced
5ml/1 tsp chopped galangal
1 large red chilli, seeded and finely sliced
2 spring onions, finely sliced
10–12 mint leaves, torn
1 head of lettuce, to serve
sprigs of coriander and 2 red chillies, seeded and sliced, to garnish

SERVES 4–6

1 Trim the chicken breasts of any excess fat and put them in a large dish. Rub with the garlic, soy sauce and 15ml/1 tbsp of the oil. Leave to marinate for 1–2 hours.

2 Grill or pan-fry the chicken for 3–4 minutes on both sides or until cooked. Remove and set aside to cool.

3 In a small saucepan, heat the coconut cream, fish sauce, lime juice and palm sugar. Stir until all of the sugar has dissolved and then remove from the heat.

4 Cut the cooked chicken into strips and combine with the water chestnuts, cashew nuts, shallots, kaffir lime leaves, lemon grass, galangal, red chilli, spring onions and mint leaves.

5 Pour the coconut dressing over the chicken, toss and mix well. Serve the chicken on a bed of lettuce leaves and garnish with sprigs of coriander and sliced red chillies.

CHIANG MAI SALAD

Chiang Mai is a city in the north-east of Thailand. The city is culturally very close to Laos and famous for its chicken salad, which was originally called "Laap" or "Larp". Duck, beef or pork can be used instead of chicken.

INGREDIENTS
450g/1lb minced chicken
1 lemon grass stalk, finely chopped
3 kaffir lime leaves, finely chopped
4 red chillies, seeded and chopped
60ml/4 tbsp lime juice
30ml/2 tbsp fish sauce
15ml/1 tbsp roasted ground rice
2 spring onions, chopped
30ml/2 tbsp coriander leaves
mixed salad leaves, to serve
cucumber and tomato slices, and a few
sprigs of mint, to garnish

SERVES 4–6

1 Heat a large non-stick frying pan. Add the minced chicken and a little water to moisten while cooking.

2 Stir constantly until cooked; this will take about 7–10 minutes.

3 Transfer the cooked chicken to a large bowl and add the rest of the ingredients. Mix thoroughly.

4 Serve on a bed of mixed salad leaves and garnish with cucumber, tomato slices and a few sprigs of mint.

COOK'S TIP
Use sticky, or glutinous, rice to make roasted ground rice. Put the rice in a frying pan and dry-roast until golden brown. Remove and grind to a powder in a pestle and mortar or in a food processor. Keep in a glass jar in a cool and dry place and use as required.

HOT AND SOUR CHICKEN SALAD

A delicious substantial salad from Vietnam, known as *Nuong Ngu Vi*, with a piquant peanut flavour.

INGREDIENTS
2 chicken breast fillets, skinned
1 small red chilli, seeded and
finely chopped
1 piece fresh root ginger, 1cm/½in long,
peeled and finely chopped
1 clove garlic, crushed
15ml/1 tbsp crunchy peanut butter
30ml/2 tbsp chopped coriander leaves
5ml/1 tsp sugar
2.5ml/½ tsp salt
15ml/1 tbsp rice or white wine vinegar
60ml/4 tbsp vegetable oil
10ml/2 tsp fish sauce (optional)

FOR THE SALAD
115g/4oz beansprouts
1 head Chinese leaves, roughly shredded
2 medium carrots, cut into thin sticks
1 red onion, cut into fine rings
2 large gherkins, sliced

SERVES 4–6

1 Slice the chicken thinly, place in a shallow bowl and set aside. Grind the chilli, ginger and garlic in a pestle and mortar. Transfer to a small bowl and add the peanut butter, coriander leaves, sugar and salt. Mix thoroughly.

2 Add the vinegar, 2 tablespoons of the oil and the fish sauce, if using, to the small bowl. Combine well. Brush this spice mixture all over the chicken strips and leave to marinate in a cool place for at least 2–3 hours, until the flavours have soaked into the meat.

3 Heat the remaining 2 tablespoons of oil in a wok or deep frying pan. Add the chicken to the hot oil and cook for 10–12 minutes, tossing the meat occasionally. Serve hot, arranged with the salad.

BALINESE SPICED DUCK

D uck is a popular ingredient all over Asia. Cooked Balinese-style, in coconut milk and spices, it is deliciously moist and tender.

INGREDIENTS
8 duck portions, fat trimmed and reserved
50g/2oz/¹/₄ cup desiccated coconut
175ml/6fl oz/³/₄ cup coconut milk
salt and freshly ground black pepper
deep-fried onions, to garnish
salad and chopped herbs, to serve

FOR THE SPICE PASTE
1 small onion or 4–6 shallots, sliced
2 garlic cloves, sliced
1cm/¹/₂ in fresh root ginger,
peeled and sliced
1cm/¹/₂ in fresh lengkuas,
peeled and sliced
2.5cm/1in fresh turmeric or 2.5ml/¹/₂ tsp
ground turmeric
1–2 red chillies, seeded and sliced
4 macadamia nuts or 8 almonds
5ml/1 tsp coriander seeds, dry-fried

SERVES 4

1 Place the duck fat trimmings in a heated frying pan, without oil, and allow the fat to drip off. Reserve the fat.

2 Fry the desiccated coconut in a preheated pan without oil, until crisp and brown in colour.

3 To make the spice paste, blend the onion or shallots, garlic, ginger, *lengkuas*, fresh or ground turmeric, chillies, nuts and coriander seeds to a paste in a food processor or with a pestle and mortar.

4 Spread half the spice paste over the duck portions and leave to marinate in a cool place for 3–4 hours. Preheat the oven to 160°C/325°F/Gas 3. Transfer the duck breasts to an oiled roasting tin. Cover with a double layer of foil and cook the duck in the oven for about 2 hours. When cooked, remove the duck from the pan and set aside to keep warm. Reserve the fat and juices from the duck and keep in the pan.

5 Turn the oven temperature up to 190°C/375°F/Gas 5. Heat the reserved duck fat in a pan, add the remaining spice paste and fry for 1–2 minutes. Stir in the coconut milk and simmer for 2 minutes. Cover the duck with the spice mixture and sprinkle with the fried coconut. Cook in the oven for 20–30 minutes.

6 Arrange the duck on a platter and garnish with deep-fried onions. Season to taste and serve with the salad and herbs.

CRISPY AROMATIC DUCK

Because this dish is often served with pancakes, spring onions, cucumber and duck sauce or plum sauce, many people mistakenly think it is Peking duck. This recipe, however, uses quite a different cooking method. The result is just as crispy but the delightful aroma makes this dish particularly distinctive. Thin pancakes are widely available from Chinese supermarkets and delicatessens.

INGREDIENTS

1 oven-ready duckling, weighing about
1.75–2.25kg/4½–5lb
10ml/2 tsp salt
5–6 whole star anise
15ml/1 tbsp Szechuan peppercorns
5ml/1 tsp cloves
2–3 cinnamon sticks
3–4 spring onions
3–4 slices fresh root ginger, unpeeled
75–90ml/5–6 tbsp Chinese rice wine or dry sherry
vegetable oil, for deep-frying
lettuce leaves, to garnish
12–16 thin pancakes, plum sauce,
½ bunch shredded spring onions,
½ cucumber cut into matchstick strips, to serve

SERVES 6–8

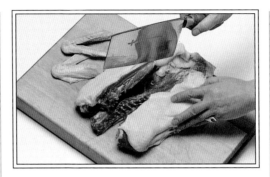

1 Remove the wings from the duck. Split the body in half down the backbone. Rub salt all over the two duck halves, taking care to rub it well in. Place the duck in a dish with the spices, the spring onions, root ginger and rice wine or sherry. Leave the duck to marinate for at least 4–6 hours, turning occasionally.

2 Steam the duck vigorously with the marinade for 3–4 hours (longer if possible), then remove from the cooking liquid and leave to cool, covered, for at least 5–6 hours. The duck must be completely cold and dry or the skin will not be crispy.

3 Heat the oil in a wok until smoking, place the duck pieces in the oil, skin-side down, and deep-fry for 5–6 minutes or until crisp and brown, turning just once at the very last moment.

4 Remove the duck from the wok with a slotted spoon and drain on kitchen paper. Arrange the lettuce leaves on a large platter. To serve, place the duck on the lettuce and remove from the bone at the table or before serving. Each guest places a few pieces of meat on a pancake, adds some sauce, spring onion and cucumber, then rolls up the pancake.

STIR-FRIED TURKEY WITH MANGE-TOUTS

The crunchiness of the mange-touts, water chestnuts, spring onions and cashew nuts gives this Chinese turkey dish an interesting texture.

INGREDIENTS

30ml/2 tbsp sesame oil
90ml/6 tbsp lemon juice
1 garlic clove, crushed
1cm/½in piece fresh root ginger, peeled and grated
5ml/1 tsp clear honey
450ml/1lb turkey fillets, cut into strips
115g/4oz mange-touts, trimmed
30ml/2 tbsp groundnut oil
50g/2oz/½ cup cashew nuts
6 spring onions, cut into strips
225g/8oz can water chestnuts, drained and thinly sliced
salt
saffron rice, to serve

SERVES 4

1 Mix together the sesame oil, lemon juice, garlic, ginger and honey in a shallow non-metallic dish. Add the turkey and mix well. Cover and leave to marinate for 3–4 hours stirring occasionally.

2 Blanch the mange-touts in boiling salted water for 1 minute. Drain and refresh under cold running water.

3 Drain the marinade from the turkey strips and reserve the marinade. Heat the groundnut oil in a wok or large frying pan, add the cashew nuts and stir-fry for about 1–2 minutes until golden brown. Using a slotted spoon, remove the cashew nuts from the wok and set them aside.

4 Add the turkey strips to the wok and stir-fry for 3–4 minutes, until they are golden brown on all sides. Add the spring onions, mange-touts and water chestnuts and pour in the reserved marinade. Cook for a few minutes, until the turkey is tender and the sauce is bubbling and hot.

5 Return the nuts to the wok and stir in. Transfer to a warmed serving platter and serve immediately, with saffron rice.

CHICKEN AND VEGETABLE STIR-FRY

Make this quick supper dish a little hotter and spicier by adding either more fresh root ginger or oyster sauce, if you wish.

INGREDIENTS
rind of ½ lemon
1cm/½in piece of fresh root ginger
1 large garlic clove
30ml/2 tbsp sunflower oil
275g/10oz lean chicken, thinly sliced
½ red pepper, seeded and sliced
½ green pepper, seeded and sliced
4 spring onions, chopped
2 carrots, cut into matchsticks
115g/4oz fine French beans
30ml/2 tbsp oyster sauce
pinch of sugar
25g/1oz/¼ cup salted peanuts,
lightly crushed
salt and ground black pepper
fresh coriander leaves, to garnish
rice, to serve

SERVES 4

1 Thinly slice the lemon rind. Peel and chop the ginger and garlic. Heat the oil in a frying pan or wok over a high heat. Add the lemon rind, ginger and garlic, and stir-fry for 30 seconds until brown.

2 Add the chicken and stir-fry for about 2 minutes. Add the vegetables *(left)* and stir-fry for 4–5 minutes, until the chicken is cooked and the vegetables are tender.

3 Finally stir in the oyster sauce, sugar, peanuts and seasoning to taste and stir-fry for another minute to mix and blend well. Serve at once, sprinkled with the coriander leaves and accompanied with rice.

CHICKEN WITH CHINESE VEGETABLES

T he chicken in this recipe can be replaced by almost any other meat, such as pork, beef or liver – or you can even use prawns, if you prefer.

INGREDIENTS
225–275g/8–10oz chicken, boned and skinned
5ml/1 tsp salt
½ egg white, lightly beaten
10ml/2 tsp cornflour, mixed with a little water
60ml/4 tbsp vegetable oil
6–8 small dried shiitake mushrooms, soaked
115g/4oz sliced bamboo shoots, drained
115g/4oz mange-touts, trimmed
1 spring onion, cut into short sections
a few small pieces fresh root ginger, peeled
5ml/1 tsp light brown sugar
15ml/1 tbsp light soy sauce
15ml/1 tbsp Chinese rice wine or dry sherry
few drops of sesame oil, to serve

SERVES 4

1 Cut the chicken into thin 2.5cm/1in slices. In a bowl, mix a pinch of the salt with the egg white and cornflour paste.

2 Heat a wok, then add the oil. When it is hot, add the chicken slices and stir-fry over a medium heat for about 30 seconds, then, using a slotted spoon, transfer to a plate and keep warm.

3 Add the mushrooms, bamboo shoots, mange-touts, spring onion and ginger and stir-fry over a high heat for about 1 minute. Add the salt, sugar, and chicken. Blend together, then add the soy sauce and wine or sherry. Stir a few more times, then sprinkle with the sesame oil and serve.

KUNG PO CHICKEN, SZECHUAN STYLE

K ung Po was the name of a court official in Szechuan; his cook created this dish. Omit some or all of the chillies for a less spicy dish.

INGREDIENTS

350g/12oz chicken thighs, skinned
and boned
1.5ml/¼ tsp salt
½ egg white, lightly beaten
10ml/2 tsp cornflour, mixed with water
1 green pepper, cored and seeded
60ml/4 tbsp vegetable oil
3–4 whole dried red chillies, soaked in
water for 10 minutes
1 spring onion, cut into short sections
few small pieces of fresh root
ginger, peeled
15ml/1 tbsp sweet bean paste or
hoi-sin sauce
5ml/1 tsp hot bean paste
15ml/1 tbsp Chinese rice wine or
dry sherry
115g/4oz/1 cup roasted cashew nuts and
a few drops of sesame oil, to serve

SERVES 4

1 Cut the chicken into 1cm/½in cubes. In a bowl, mix the chicken with the salt, egg white and cornflour paste. Cut the green pepper into squares about the same size as the chicken cubes.

2 Heat a wok, then add the oil. When it is hot, add the chicken cubes and stir-fry for about 1 minute, or until the colour changes. Remove the chicken from the wok with a slotted spoon and keep warm.

3 Add the green pepper, soaked red chillies, spring onion and ginger and stir-fry for about 1 minute.

4 Add the chicken to the wok with the sweet bean paste or hoi-sin sauce, hot bean paste and wine or sherry. Blend thoroughly and cook for 1 further minute. Finally stir in the cashew nuts and sesame oil. Transfer to a warmed serving platter and serve immediately.

SOY-BRAISED CHICKEN

This dish can be served hot or cold. Soy sauce is a vital ingredient in Chinese cooking. Light soy sauce is thinner and saltier than dark.

INGREDIENTS
1 whole chicken, weighing about
1.5kg/3–3½lb
15ml/1 tbsp ground Szechuan
peppercorns
30ml/2 tbsp finely chopped fresh
root ginger
45ml/3 tbsp light soy sauce
30ml/2 tbsp dark soy sauce
45ml/3 tbsp Chinese rice wine or sherry
15ml/1 tbsp light brown sugar
vegetable oil, for deep-frying
600ml/1 pint/2½ cups chicken stock
or water
10ml/2 tsp salt
25g/1oz/2 tbsp sugar
lettuce leaves, to garnish

SERVES 6–8

1 Rub the chicken, both inside and out, with the Szechuan pepper and ginger. Marinate the bird with the soy sauces, wine or sherry and sugar for 3 hours, turning the bird several times.

2 Heat a wok, then add the oil. When it is hot, add the chicken, reserving the marinade, and deep-fry for 5–6 minutes, or until brown all over.

3 Remove and drain. Pour off the excess oil, add the marinade with the stock or water, salt and the sugar and bring to the boil. Return the chicken to the wok and braise in the sauce, covered, for 35–40 minutes, turning once or twice.

4 Remove the chicken and let it cool a little before chopping it into about 30 bite-size pieces. Arrange the chicken pieces on a bed of lettuce leaves, then pour some of the sauce over and serve at once. Use the remaining sauce another time.

Meat Dishes

Spices have the dual effect of flavouring and tenderizing meat. This makes Indian dishes such as Lentils with Lamb and Tomatoes tender to the taste and redolent with the flavours of turmeric, chilli, cinnamon and coriander.

Until quite recently, meat did not play a large part in Asian cuisines, in part for religious or legal reasons and because land was scarce there were few places to graze livestock.

Today meat is one of many ingredients in a dish rather than being the sole ingredient. In Chinese and Japanese dishes the meat is cooked simply and for the minimum of time, requiring good quality, lean cuts of meat. The flavours of orange, ginger, soy sauce, mooli and dashi or Szechuan peppercorns augment the taste.

Meat curries, by contrast, combine numerous ingredients with rich sauces. Mussaman Curry from Thailand uses a curry paste of that name full of chilli, garlic, lemon grass, galangal and various seeds and spices. The paste can be stored for four months and used with this dish which features steak, potatoes, peanuts and coconut, or with other ingredients of your choice.

LAMB WITH SPINACH

L amb with Spinach is a well-known recipe from the Punjab region. It is important to use red peppers as they add such a distinctive flavour to the finished dish.

INGREDIENTS

5ml/1 tsp sliced fresh root ginger
1 garlic clove, crushed
7.5ml/1½ tsp chilli powder
5ml/1 tsp salt
5ml/1 tsp garam masala
90ml/6 tbsp corn oil
2 onions, sliced
675g/1½lb lean lamb, cut into
5cm/2in cubes
600–900ml/1–1½ pints/2½–3¾ cups water
400g/14oz fresh spinach
1 large red pepper, seeded and chopped
3 fresh green chillies, chopped
45ml/3 tbsp chopped fresh coriander
15ml/1 tbsp lemon juice (optional)

SERVES 4–6

COOK'S TIP
Frozen spinach can also be used for this dish, but try to find whole leaf spinach rather than the chopped kind – it has a much better flavour.

1 Mix together the ginger, garlic, chilli powder, salt and garam masala in a bowl. Set aside.

2 Heat the oil in a saucepan, add the onions and fry for 10–12 minutes or until well browned. Add the lamb pieces and stir-fry for about 2 minutes.

3 Add the spice mixture and stir thoroughly until the lamb is well coated. Pour in the water and bring to the boil, then cover the pan and lower the heat. Cook gently for 25–35 minutes without letting the contents of the pan burn. If there is still a lot of water remaining in the pan remove the lid and boil briskly to evaporate the excess.

4 Meanwhile, wash and roughly chop the spinach, discarding any tough stalks, then blanch it for about 1 minute in a pan of boiling water. Drain well.

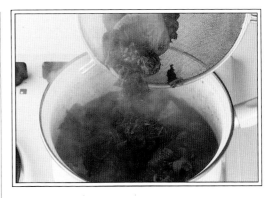

5 Add the spinach to the lamb and cook for 7–10 minutes, using a wooden spoon in a semi-circular motion, scraping the bottom of the pan as you stir.

6 Add the red pepper, green chillies and chopped fresh coriander to the pan and stir over a moderate heat for 2 minutes. Sprinkle with the lemon juice, if using, and serve immediately. Serve with a simple accompaniment such as plain boiled rice or Naan Bread.

KHARA MASALA LAMB

Whole spices (*khara*) are used in this curry so you should warn your guests. It is delicious with freshly baked Naan Bread or boiled rice.

INGREDIENTS

75ml/5 tbsp corn oil
2 onions, chopped
5ml/1 tsp sliced fresh root ginger
1 garlic clove, sliced
6 dried red chillies
3 cardamom pods
2 cinnamon sticks
6 black peppercorns
3 cloves
2.5ml/½ tsp salt
450g/1lb boned leg of lamb, cubed
600ml/1 pint/2½ cups water
2 fresh green chillies, sliced
30ml/2 tbsp chopped fresh coriander

SERVES 4

COOK'S TIP
The technique of stirring the meat and spices with a semi-circular motion, used in step 3, is called *bhoonoing*. It ensures that the meat is well coated with the spice mixture before the cooking liquid is added.

1 Heat the oil in a large saucepan, lower the heat slightly, add the onions, and fry until they are lightly browned.

2 Add half of the ginger and half of the garlic and stir well. Add half of the red chillies, the cardamom pods, cinnamon, peppercorns, cloves and salt.

3 Add the lamb and fry over a moderate heat. Stir constantly for 5 minutes with a semi-circular movement, using a wooden spoon to scrape the bottom of the pan.

4 Pour in the water, cover with a lid and cook over a moderately low heat for 35–40 minutes, or until the water has evaporated and the meat is tender.

5 Add the remaining ginger, garlic and dried red chillies to the pan, then stir in the fresh green chillies and the chopped fresh coriander.

6 Continue cooking, stirring constantly, until you see some free oil on the sides of the pan. Transfer to a warmed serving dish and serve immediately.

BALTI LAMB-STUFFED VEGETABLES

ubergines and peppers make a good combination. Here they are stuffed with an aromatic lamb filling.

INGREDIENTS
3 small aubergines
1 each red, green and yellow pepper

FOR THE STUFFING
45ml/3 tbsp corn oil
3 onions, sliced
5ml/1 tsp chilli powder
1.5ml/¼ tsp turmeric
5ml/1 tsp ground coriander
5ml/1 tsp ground cumin
1 garlic clove, crushed
5ml/1 tsp salt
450g/1lb lean minced lamb
30ml/2 tbsp chopped fresh coriander

FOR THE SAUTEED ONIONS
45ml/3 tbsp corn oil
5ml/1 tsp mixed onion, mustard,
fenugreek and white cumin seeds
4 dried red chillies
3 onions, roughly chopped
5ml/1 tsp salt
2 tomatoes, sliced
2 fresh green chillies, chopped
30ml/2 tbsp chopped fresh coriander

SERVES 6

1 Prepare the vegetables. Slit the aubergines lengthways up to the stalks, leaving the stalks intact. Cut the tops off the peppers and scoop out the seeds. You can keep the pepper tops to use as 'lids' for the stuffed vegetables, if wished.

2 To make the stuffing, heat the oil in a saucepan. Add the onions and fry for about 3 minutes. Lower the heat and add the chilli powder, turmeric, ground coriander, ground cumin, garlic and salt, and stir-fry for about 1 minute. Add the minced lamb and turn up the heat.

3 Stir-fry for 7–10 minutes, or until the mince is cooked. Add the fresh coriander towards the end of the cooking time and stir to mix. Remove the mince mixture from the heat, cover and set aside.

4 Make the sautéed onions. Heat the oil in a deep round-bottomed frying pan or a karahi and add the mixed onion, mustard, fenugreek and white cumin seeds and red chillies and fry for 1 minute. Add the onions and fry for 2 minutes or until soft.

5 Add the salt, sliced tomatoes, chopped green chillies and the chopped fresh coriander and cook for 1 further minute. Remove from the heat and set aside.

6 When the minced lamb mixture is cool, stuff the aubergines and peppers. Using a small spoon, fill them quite loosely with the meat mixture.

7 Place the stuffed vegetables on top of the sautéed onions in the karahi. Cover with foil, making sure the foil doesn't touch the food, and cook over a low heat for about 15 minutes, until the aubergines and peppers are tender. Serve with a dish of plain boiled rice or Colourful Pullao Rice.

COOK'S TIP
Large beef tomatoes are also delicious stuffed with this lightly spiced lamb mixture. Simply cut off the tops and scoop out the cores, seeds and some of the pulp and cook as above.

LENTILS WITH LAMB AND TOMATOES

This aromatically spiced dish is rich in protein and has a deliciously light texture. Colourful Pullao Rice makes a perfect accompaniment.

INGREDIENTS
60ml/4 tbsp corn oil
2 bay leaves
2 cloves
4 black peppercorns
1 onion, sliced
450g/1lb lean lamb, boned and cubed
1.5ml/¼ tsp ground turmeric
7.5ml/1½ tsp chilli powder
5ml/1 tsp crushed coriander seeds
2.5cm/1in piece cinnamon stick
1 garlic clove, crushed
7.5ml/1½ tsp salt
1.5 litres/2½ pints/6¼ cups water
50g/2oz/⅓ cup chana dhal (split yellow lentils) or yellow split peas
2 tomatoes, quartered
2 fresh green chillies, chopped
15ml/1 tbsp chopped fresh coriander

SERVES 4

1 Heat the oil in a deep round-bottomed frying pan or a karahi. Lower the heat slightly and add the bay leaves, cloves, peppercorns and onion and fry for about 5 minutes, or until the onions are golden.

2 Add the lamb cubes, ground turmeric, chilli powder, coriander seeds, cinnamon stick, garlic and most of the salt to the pan. Stir-fry the lamb mixture for about 5 minutes over a moderate heat.

3 Pour in 900ml/1½ pints/3¾ cups of the water and cover the pan with a lid or foil, making sure the foil does not come into contact with the contents of the pan. Simmer the lamb over a low heat for about 35–40 minutes, or until the water has evaporated and the lamb is tender.

4 Meanwhile, put the lentils into a saucepan with the remaining 600ml/ 1 pint/2½ cups water and boil for about 12–15 minutes, or until the water has almost evaporated and the lentils are soft enough to mash easily. If the lentil mixture is too thick, gradually add up to 150ml/¼ pint/⅔ cup water until they mash easily.

5 When the lamb is tender, stir-fry the mixture using a wooden spoon, until some free oil begins to appear on the sides of the pan.

6 Add the cooked lentils to the lamb and mix together well with a wooden spoon.

7 Stir in the tomatoes, chillies and fresh coriander then transfer to a warmed serving dish and serve immediately.

VARIATION
Boned and cubed chicken can be used in place of the lamb. At step 3, reduce the amount of water to 300ml/½ pint/ 1¼ cups and cook uncovered, stirring occasionally, for 10–15 minutes or until the water has evaporated and the chicken is cooked through.

MUSSAMAN CURRY

This curry is Indian in origin. Traditionally it is made with beef, but chicken or lamb can be used, or you can make a vegetarian version using tofu. It has a rich, sweet and spicy flavour. Serve with boiled rice.

INGREDIENTS
600ml/1 pint/2½ cups coconut milk
675g/1½lb stewing steak, cut into
2.5cm/1in chunks
250ml/8fl oz/1 cup coconut cream
45ml/3 tbsp Mussaman curry paste
(see Cook's Tip)
30ml/2 tbsp fish sauce
15ml/1 tbsp palm sugar
60ml/4 tbsp tamarind juice
6 cardamom pods
1 cinnamon stick
225g/8oz potatoes, cut into
even-size chunks
1 onion, cut into wedges
50g/2oz roasted peanuts
boiled rice, to serve

SERVES 4–6

1 Bring the coconut milk to a gentle boil in a large saucepan. Add the beef and simmer for about 40 minutes, until tender.

2 Put the coconut cream into a saucepan, then cook for about 5–8 minutes, stirring constantly, until it separates.

3 Add the Mussaman curry paste and fry until fragrant. Add the fried curry paste to the pan containing the cooked beef.

4 Add the fish sauce, sugar, tamarind juice, cardamom pods, cinnamon stick, potato chunks and onion. Simmer until the potatoes are cooked, for 10–15 minutes.

5 Add the roasted peanuts. Cook for a further 5 minutes, then serve with rice.

COOK'S TIP
Mussaman curry paste is used to make the Thai version of a Muslim curry. It can be prepared and then stored in a glass jar in the fridge for up to four months.
Remove the seeds from 12 large dried chillies and soak in hot water for 15 minutes. Combine 60ml/4 tbsp chopped shallots, 5 garlic cloves, 1 chopped lemon grass stalk, 10ml/2 tsp chopped galangal, 5ml/1 tsp cumin seeds, 15ml/1 tbsp coriander seeds, 2 cloves and 6 black peppercorns. Place in a wok and dry-fry over a low heat for 5–6 minutes. Grind or process into a powder and stir in 5ml/1 tsp shrimp paste, 5ml/1 tsp salt, 5ml/1 tsp sugar and 30ml/2 tbsp oil.

FRAGRANT THAI MEATBALLS

A creamy peanut sauce accompanies these tasty little meatballs, which can be made of beef or pork.

INGREDIENTS
450g/1lb lean minced pork or beef
15ml/1 tbsp chopped garlic
1 lemon grass stalk, finely chopped
4 spring onions, finely chopped
15ml/1 tbsp chopped fresh coriander
30ml/2 tbsp red curry paste
15ml/1 tbsp lemon juice
15ml/1 tbsp fish sauce
1 egg
salt and freshly ground black pepper
rice flour, for dusting
oil, for deep frying
sprigs of coriander, to garnish

FOR THE PEANUT SAUCE
15ml/1 tbsp vegetable oil
15ml/1 tbsp red curry paste
30ml/2 tbsp crunchy peanut butter
15ml/1 tbsp palm sugar
15ml/1 tbsp lemon juice
250ml/8fl oz/1 cup coconut milk

SERVES 4–6

1 Make the peanut sauce. Heat the oil in a small saucepan, add the curry paste and fry for 1 minute.

2 Stir in the rest of the sauce ingredients and bring to the boil. Lower the heat and simmer for 5 minutes, until the sauce has thickened.

3 Make the meatballs. Combine all the ingredients except for the rice flour, oil and coriander, and add some seasoning. Mix and blend everything together well.

4 Roll and shape the meat into small balls about the size of a walnut. Dust the meatballs with rice flour.

5 Heat the oil in a wok until hot and deep fry the meatballs in batches until nicely browned and cooked through. Drain them on kitchen paper. Serve garnished with sprigs of coriander and accompanied by the peanut sauce.

STIR-FRIED BEEF IN OYSTER SAUCE

A nother simple but delicious recipe. In Thailand fresh straw mushrooms are readily available, but oyster mushrooms make a good substitute. To make the dish even more interesting, use several types of mushroom.

INGREDIENTS
450g/1lb rump steak
30ml/2 tbsp soy sauce
15ml/1 tbsp cornflour
45ml/3 tbsp vegetable oil
15ml/1 tbsp chopped garlic
15ml/1 tbsp chopped root ginger
225g/8oz mixed mushrooms, such as shiitake, oyster and straw
30ml/2 tbsp oyster sauce
5ml/1 tsp granulated sugar
4 spring onions, cut into short lengths
freshly ground black pepper
2 red chillies, cut into strips, to garnish

SERVES 4–6

COOK'S TIP
Made from extracts of oysters, oyster sauce is velvety smooth and has a savoury-sweet and meaty taste. There are several types available; buy the best you can afford.

1 Slice the beef, on the diagonal, into long thin strips. Mix together the soy sauce and cornflour in a large bowl, stir in the beef and leave to marinate for 1–2 hours.

2 Heat half the oil in a wok or frying pan. Add the garlic and ginger and fry until fragrant. Stir in the strips of beef. Stir to separate the pieces, allow them to colour and cook for 1–2 minutes. Remove from the pan and set aside.

3 Heat the remaining oil in the wok. Add your selection of mushrooms, and cook until tender.

4 Return the beef to the wok with the mushrooms. Add the oyster sauce, sugar and freshly ground black pepper to taste. Mix well.

5 Add the spring onions. Mix together. Serve garnished with strips of red chilli.

GREEN BEEF CURRY WITH THAI AUBERGINE

his is a very quick curry to make, so be sure to use tender, good-quality meat.

INGREDIENTS
45ml/3 tbsp vegetable oil
600ml/1 pint/2½ cups coconut milk
450g/1lb beef sirloin
4 kaffir lime leaves, torn
15–30ml/1–2 tbsp fish sauce
5ml/1 tsp palm sugar
150g/5oz small Thai aubergines, halved
a small handful of Thai basil
2 green chillies, shredded to garnish

FOR THE GREEN CURRY PASTE
15 hot green chillies
2 lemon grass stalks, chopped
3 shallots, sliced
2 garlic cloves
15ml/1 tbsp chopped galangal
4 kaffir lime leaves, chopped
2.5ml/½ tsp grated kaffir lime rind
5ml/1 tsp chopped coriander root
6 black peppercorns
5ml/1 tsp coriander seeds, roasted
5ml/1 tsp cumin seeds, roasted
15ml/1 tbsp sugar
5ml/1 tsp salt
5ml/1 tsp shrimp paste (optional)

SERVES 4–6

1 Make the green curry paste. Combine all the ingredients together thoroughly. Pound them in a pestle and mortar or process in a food processor until smooth. Add 30ml/2 tbsp of the oil, a little at a time, and blend well between each addition. Keep in a glass jar in the fridge until required.

2 Heat the remaining oil in a large saucepan or wok. Add 45ml/3 tbsp green curry paste and fry until fragrant.

3 Stir in half the coconut milk, a little at a time. Cook for about 5–6 minutes, until an oily sheen appears.

4 Cut the beef into long thin slices and add to the saucepan with the kaffir lime leaves, fish sauce, sugar and aubergines. Cook for 2–3 minutes, then stir in the remaining coconut milk.

5 Bring back to a simmer and cook until the meat and aubergines are tender. Stir in the Thai basil just before serving. Garnish with the shredded green chillies.

THAI BEEF SALAD

A hearty salad of beef, laced with a chilli and lime dressing that perfectly complements the meat.

INGREDIENTS
2 × 225g/8oz sirloin steaks
1 red onion, finely sliced
½ cucumber, cut into thin ribbons
1 lemon grass stalk, finely chopped
30ml/2 tbsp chopped spring onions
juice of 2 limes
15–30ml/1–2 tbsp fish sauce
2–4 red chillies, finely sliced, fresh coriander, Chinese mustard cress and mint leaves, to garnish

SERVES 4

1 Pan-fry or grill the sirloin steaks to medium-rare. Set aside to rest for about 10–15 minutes.

2 When cool, thinly slice the beef and put the slices in a large bowl.

3 Add the sliced onion, cucumber ribbons and lemon grass.

4 Add the spring onions. Toss and season with lime juice and fish sauce. Serve at room temperature or chilled, garnished with the sliced chillies, coriander, Chinese mustard cress and mint leaves.

SWEET AND SOUR PORK, THAI-STYLE

Sweet and sour is traditionally a Chinese creation but the Thais also do it very well. This version has an altogether fresher and cleaner flavour and it makes a good one-dish meal when served over rice.

INGREDIENTS
350g/12oz lean pork
30ml/2 tbsp vegetable oil
4 garlic cloves, finely sliced
1 small red onion, sliced
30ml/2 tbsp fish sauce
15ml/1 tbsp granulated sugar
1 red pepper, seeded and diced
½ cucumber, seeded and sliced
2 plum tomatoes, cut into wedges
115g/4oz pineapple, cut into
small chunks
2 spring onions, cut into short lengths
freshly ground black pepper
coriander leaves and spring onions,
shredded, to garnish

SERVES 4

1 Slice the pork into thin strips. Heat the oil in a wok or large frying pan.

2 Add the garlic and fry until golden, then add the pork and stir-fry for about 4–5 minutes. Add the onion.

3 Season with fish sauce, sugar and freshly ground black pepper. Stir and cook for 3–4 minutes, or until the pork is cooked.

4 Add the rest of the vegetables, the pineapple and spring onions. You may need to add a few tablespoons of water. Continue to stir-fry for another 3–4 minutes. Serve hot, garnished with coriander leaves and spring onions.

RENDANG

This popular Indonesian dish is often served with deep-fried onions and plain boiled rice.

INGREDIENTS

1kg/2¼lb prime beef in one piece
2 onions or 5–6 shallots, sliced
4 garlic cloves, crushed
2.5cm/1in fresh lengkuas, peeled and sliced, or 5ml/1 tsp lengkuas powder
2.5cm/1in fresh root ginger, peeled and sliced
4–6 fresh red chillies, seeded and sliced
1 lemon grass stem, lower part, sliced
2.5cm/1in fresh turmeric, peeled and sliced, or 5ml/1 tsp ground turmeric
5ml/1 tsp coriander seeds, dry-fried and ground
5ml/1 tsp cumin seeds, dry-fried and ground
2 kaffir lime leaves
5ml/1 tsp tamarind pulp, soaked in 60ml/4 tbsp warm water
2 x 400ml/14fl oz cans coconut milk
300ml/½ pint/1¼ cups water
30ml/2 tbsp dark soy sauce
6–8 small new potatoes, scrubbed
salt
boiled rice and deep-fried onions, to serve

1 Cut the meat in long strips and then into even-size pieces and place in a bowl.

2 Process the onions or shallots, crushed garlic, lengkuas or lengkuas powder, sliced ginger, chopped and deseeded chillies, sliced lemon grass and the fresh or ground turmeric to a fine paste in a food processor. Alternatively, grind finely together using a pestle and mortar.

COOK'S TIP
This dish tastes even better and more flavoursome if cooked a day in advance. Follow the recipe up to the end of Step 5; on the next day reheat and add the potatoes and seasoning.

3 Add the paste to the meat with the coriander and cumin and mix well. Tear the lime leaves and add them to the mixture. Cover and leave in a cool place to marinate while you prepare the other ingredients.

4 Strain the tamarind and reserve the juice. Pour the coconut milk, water and tamarind juice into a wok or flameproof casserole and stir in the spiced meat and soy sauce. Add seasoning as desired.

5 Stir until the liquid comes to the boil; then reduce the heat and simmer gently, half-covered, for about 1½–2 hours or until the meat is tender and the liquid reduced.

6 Add the potatoes 20–25 minutes before the end of the cooking time. Add a little more water to the pot. Season to taste and serve with rice and deep-fried onions.

STIR-FRIED BEEF WITH ORANGE AND GINGER

Stir-frying uses the minimum of fat and it's also one of the quickest ways to cook, but you do need to choose very tender meat.

INGREDIENTS
450g/1lb lean beef rump, fillet or sirloin, cut into thin strips
finely grated rind and juice of 1 orange
15ml/1 tbsp light soy sauce
5ml/1 tsp cornflour
2.5cm/1in piece fresh root ginger, finely chopped
10ml/2 tsp sesame oil
1 large carrot, cut into thin strips
2 spring onions, thinly sliced
rice noodles or boiled rice, to serve

SERVES 4

1 Place the beef strips in a bowl and sprinkle over the orange rind and juice. Cover and leave to marinate for at least 30 minutes, stirring from time to time.

2 Drain the marinade from the meat and reserve the marinade. Mix the meat with the soy sauce, cornflour and ginger.

3 Heat the sesame oil in a wok or large frying pan. When it is hot, add the beef strips and stir-fry for 1 minute until they are lightly coloured. Add the carrot strips and stir-fry for a further 2–3 minutes.

COOK'S TIP
To extract the maximum amount of juice from an orange, warm it for a short while in the oven, then roll it backwards and forwards with your hand before squeezing.

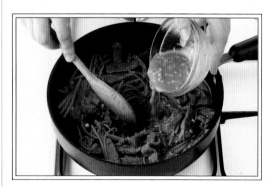

4 Stir in the sliced spring onions and the reserved marinade, then cook over a medium heat, stirring constantly, until the sauce is boiling, thickened and glossy. Serve the stir-fried beef immediately, accompanied by a serving of rice noodles, or just plain boiled rice.

DRY-FRIED SHREDDED BEEF

Dry-frying is a unique Szechuan cooking method, in which the main ingredient is first stir-fried slowly over a low heat until dry, then finished off quickly with the other ingredients over a high heat.

INGREDIENTS
350–400g/12–14oz lean beef
1 large or 2 small carrots
2–3 celery sticks
30ml/2 tbsp sesame oil
15ml/1 tbsp Chinese rice wine or dry sherry
15ml/1 tbsp hot bean sauce
15ml/1 tbsp light soy sauce
1 garlic clove, finely chopped
5ml/1 tsp light brown sugar
2–3 spring onions, finely chopped
2.5ml/½ tsp finely chopped fresh root ginger
ground Szechuan peppercorns, to taste

SERVES 4

1 Using a cleaver or a very sharp knife, slice the beef into matchstick shreds. Thinly shred the carrots and celery into pieces about the same size.

2 Heat a wok, then add the sesame oil (it will smoke very quickly). Reduce the heat and stir-fry the beef shreds with the wine or sherry until the colour changes.

3 Pour off the excess liquid from the wok and reserve. Continue stirring until the meat is absolutely dry.

4 Add the hot bean sauce, soy sauce, garlic and sugar. Blend thoroughly, then add the carrot and celery shreds.

5 Increase the heat to high and add the spring onions, ginger and the reserved cooking liquid. Continue stirring and, when all the juice has evaporated, season with Szechuan pepper and serve.

STIR-FRIED PORK WITH VEGETABLES

This is a basic recipe for cooking any meat with any vegetables in an authentic Chinese style. It can be varied according to seasonal availability.

INGREDIENTS

225g/8oz pork tenderloin
15ml/1 tbsp light soy sauce
5ml/1 tsp light brown sugar
5ml/1 tsp Chinese rice wine or dry sherry
10ml/2 tsp cornflour mixed with a little water
115g/4oz mange-touts
115g/4oz mushrooms
1 large or 2 small carrots
1 spring onion
60ml/4 tbsp vegetable oil
5ml/1 tsp salt
chicken stock or water, if necessary
few drops of sesame oil, to serve

SERVES 4

1 Cut the pork into thin 2.5cm/1in slices. Marinate with about 5ml/1 tsp of the soy sauce, the sugar, wine or sherry and cornflour paste.

2 Top and tail the mange-touts; thinly slice the mushrooms; cut the carrots into pieces roughly the same size as the pork, and cut the spring onion diagonally into short sections.

3 Heat a wok, then add the oil. When it is hot, add the pork and stir-fry for about 1 minute or until its colour changes. Remove with a slotted spoon and keep warm.

4 Put the prepared vegetables into the wok and cook, stirring and turning, for about 2 minutes.

5 Add the salt and the partly cooked pork, and a little stock or water only if necessary. Continue stirring for a further 1–2 minutes, then add the remaining soy sauce and blend thoroughly. Sprinkle with sesame oil and serve immediately.

MU SHU PORK WITH EGGS AND MUSHROOMS

I n Chinese *Mu Shu* is the name for a bright yellow flower. Traditionally, this dish is served as a filling wrapped in thin pancakes, but it can also be served on its own with plain rice.

INGREDIENTS
15g/½oz dried wood-ear mushrooms
175–225g/6–8oz pork tenderloin
225g/8oz Chinese cabbage
115g/4oz canned bamboo shoots, drained
2 spring onions
3 eggs
5ml/1 tsp salt
60ml/4 tbsp vegetable oil
15ml/1 tbsp light soy sauce
15ml/1 tbsp Chinese rice wine or dry sherry
few drops of sesame oil, to serve

SERVES 4

1 Soak the mushrooms in a bowl of cold water for 25–30 minutes, then rinse thoroughly and discard any hard stalks. Drain the mushrooms, then thinly slice. Cut the pork into matchstick pieces. Thinly shred the Chinese cabbage, bamboo shoots and spring onions.

2 Break the eggs into a bowl, add a pinch of salt, and beat. Heat a little oil in a wok, add the eggs and stir and turn gently until lightly scrambled but not at all dry. Remove, set aside and keep warm.

3 Heat the remaining oil in the wok, add the pork and stir-fry for about 1 minute, or until the colour changes. Add the mushrooms, Chinese cabbage, bamboo shoots and spring onions and stir-fry for 1 further minute, then add the remaining salt, the soy sauce, and wine or sherry.

4 Stir-fry the vegetables for 1 further minute before returning the scrambled eggs to the wok. Break up the eggs and blend in well. Sprinkle with sesame oil and serve immediately.

GINGER PORK WITH BLACK BEAN SAUCE

T he combination of the sweetness of peppers and the saltiness of preserved black beans gives this Chinese dish a wonderful, distinctive flavour.

INGREDIENTS
350g/12oz pork fillet
1 garlic clove, crushed
15ml/1 tbsp grated fresh root ginger
90ml/6 tbsp chicken stock
30ml/2 tbsp dry sherry
15ml/1 tbsp light soy sauce
5ml/1 tsp sugar
10ml/2 tsp cornflour
45ml/3 tbsp groundnut oil
2 yellow peppers, seeded and cut into strips
2 red peppers, seeded and cut into strips
1 bunch spring onions, sliced diagonally
45ml/3 tbsp preserved black beans, coarsely chopped
fresh coriander, to garnish (optional)

SERVES 4

1 Cut the pork into thin slices across the grain of the meat. Put the slices into a bowl and mix them with the garlic and ginger. Leave to marinate at room temperature for 15 minutes.

2 Blend together the stock, sherry, soy sauce, sugar and cornflour in a small bowl, then set the sauce mixture aside.

3 Heat the oil in a wok or large frying pan, add the marinated pork and stir-fry for 2–3 minutes. Add the peppers and spring onions and stir-fry for a further 2 minutes *(left)*. Add the beans and sauce mixture and cook, stirring, until thick. Serve hot, garnished with fresh coriander, if using.

STEAK BOWL

This Japanese dish looks very good at a dinner party and it is also very easy to prepare, leaving the cook with time to relax.

INGREDIENTS

1 large mild onion
1 red pepper, seeded
30ml/2 tbsp oil
30ml/2 tbsp butter
400g/14oz sirloin steak, trimmed of excess fat
60ml/4 tbsp tomato ketchup
30ml/2 tbsp Worcestershire sauce
30ml/2 tbsp chopped parsley
1kg/2¹⁄₄lb/7 cups freshly boiled Japanese rice
salt and freshly ground black pepper
bunch of watercress, to garnish

SERVES 4

1 Cut the onion and red pepper into 7–8mm/⅓in slices.

2 Heat 15ml/1 tbsp of the oil in a frying pan and cook the onion slices until golden on both sides, adding salt and pepper, then set aside.

3 Heat the remaining oil and 15ml/1 tbsp of the butter. Cook the steak over a high heat until browned on both sides, then cut it into bite-size pieces and set aside. For well-done steak, cook it over a moderate heat for 1–2 minutes on each side.

4 Mix the tomato ketchup, Worcestershire sauce and 30ml/2 tbsp water in the pan in which the steak was cooked. Stir over a moderate heat for 1 minute, mixing in the meat residue.

5 Mix the remaining butter and the chopped parsley into the hot rice. Divide among four serving bowls. Top the rice with the red pepper, onion and steak, and pour over the sauce. Garnish with watercress.

BEEF AND VEGETABLES ON A HOT PLATE

his is *Yakiniku*, a dish of beef cooked at the table – you will need a portable griddle or grill pan and you can cook a variety of different ingredients, such as chicken or fish.

INGREDIENTS

1 oak leaf lettuce
1 mooli, finely grated
oil, for cooking
400g/14oz beef topside, very thinly sliced
1 red pepper, seeded and sliced
1 green pepper, seeded and sliced
1 large mild onion, sliced into rings
4 shiitake mushrooms, stems removed
1 carrot, thinly sliced
8 raw tiger prawns, heads removed, shelled, with tails left on
soy sauce, to serve

FOR THE PONZU DIP

100ml/3¹/₂fl oz/generous ¹/₃ cup each of lemon juice, soy sauce and instant dashi

SERVES 4

1 Prepare the dip by mixing all the ingredients. Divide the dip among four small individual serving bowls. Separate the lettuce leaves and arrange them on plates.

2 Gently squeeze the grated mooli to remove any excess water. Place 15–30ml/1–2 tbsp mooli into four small individual serving bowls and pour on a little soy sauce.

3 Heat the grill or a hot plate on a thick mat to protect the table. Add a little oil and quickly grill the beef until it is cooked on both sides. Grill the peppers, onion, shiitake mushrooms, carrot and prawns at the same time.

4 To eat the food, wrap individual portions in lettuce leaves and dip them into the ponzu or mooli dip. Alternatively, the food may be dipped without being wrapped in the lettuce leaves if preferred.

COOK'S TIP
This recipe is an example of a party meal, an essential part of Japanese home entertainment. Dishes are cooked at the table so guests can participate in cooking their own food.

VEGETABLE-STUFFED BEEF ROLLS

Thinly sliced meats are used almost daily in Japanese cooking, so there are countless recipes for them. These stuffed beef rolls, or *Yahata-maki*, are very popular for picnic meals. You can roll up other vegetables in the beef, such as asparagus tips, and you can also replace the beef with pork.

INGREDIENTS
50g/2oz carrot
50g/2oz green pepper, seeded
bunch of spring onions
400g/14oz beef topside, thinly sliced
plain flour, for dusting
15ml/1 tbsp oil
fresh parsley sprigs, to garnish

FOR THE SAUCE
30ml/2 tbsp sugar
45ml/3 tbsp soy sauce
45ml/3 tbsp mirin

SERVES 4

1 Shred the carrot and green pepper into 4–5cm/1½–2in lengths. Halve the spring onions lengthways, then shred them diagonally into similar-size lengths.

2 The beef slices should be 2mm/1/12in thick, no thicker, and about 15cm/6in square. Lay a slice of beef on a chopping board and top it with carrot, green pepper and spring onion strips. Roll it up quite tightly and dust it lightly with flour. Repeat the process with the remaining beef and sliced vegetables.

3 Heat the oil in a frying pan. Add the beef rolls, placing the joins underneath to prevent them from unrolling. Fry them over a moderate heat until golden and cooked, turning occasionally.

4 Add the sauce ingredients to the frying pan and increase the heat. Roll the beef quickly to glaze the rolls.

5 Remove the rolls from the pan and halve them, cutting at a slant. Stand the rolls, with the sloping cut end facing upwards on a plate. Dress with the sauce and garnish with parsley. Serve hot or cold.

DEEP FRIED PORK STRIPS WITH SHREDDED CABBAGE

Deep fried pork is very tasty when served with soft green cabbage and a fruity sauce, known as *tonkatsu*. This dish is enjoyed throughout Japan.

INGREDIENTS
4 boneless pork loin steaks, 115g/4oz each
7.5ml/1¹⁄₂ tsp salt
freshly ground black pepper
plain flour, for coating
2 eggs, very lightly beaten
50g/2oz fresh white breadcrumbs
¹⁄₂ soft green cabbage, finely shredded
oil, for deep frying

FOR THE TONKATSU SAUCE
100ml/3¹⁄₂fl oz/generous ¹⁄₃ cup brown sauce (select a fruity brand)
45ml/3 tbsp tomato ketchup
15ml/1 tbsp sugar

SERVES 4

COOK'S TIP
Commercial Japanese *tonkatsu* sauce is available ready-prepared and it may be substituted for the sauce ingredients listed above.

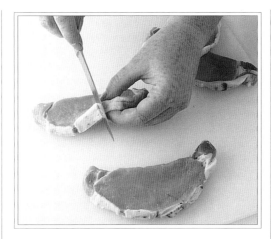

1 Snip any fat on the pork steaks to ensure that the meat remains flat when frying. Then beat the pork with a meat mallet or a rolling pin to tenderize it. Season with the salt and black pepper, and dust the pork lightly with flour.

2 Dip the steaks into the lightly beaten egg first and then coat them all over with the breadcrumbs. Press the breadcrumbs on to the steaks with your fingers to ensure they stick well. Refrigerate them for about 10 minutes, as chilling will give the coating time to set slightly.

3 Meanwhile, soak the shredded green cabbage in a bowl of cold water for about 5 minutes. Make sure that it is well drained and chill until needed.

4 Mix the ingredients for the *tonkatsu* sauce together in a bowl. Stir constantly and make sure that all the sugar has properly dissolved.

5 Slowly heat the oil for deep frying to 165–170°C/330–340°F. Deep fry two steaks at a time for about 6 minutes, turning them until they are crisp and golden.

6 Skim any floating breadcrumbs from the oil occasionally to prevent them from burning. Drain the steaks well on kitchen towels and keep hot.

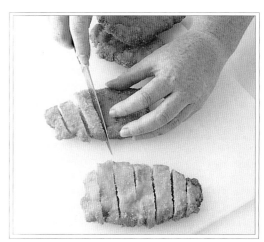

7 Cut the steaks into 2cm/³⁄₄in strips and place them on a plate. Arrange the chilled cabbage beside the pork and pour the sauce over. Serve immediately.

VEGETABLE DISHES

People who eat in Asian restaurants know about the wide variety of vegetable dishes available, making these favourite places for vegetarians to dine. Okra, spinach, potatoes, mushrooms. cauliflower and aubergines all feature highly in Indian and Balti dishes and these authentic recipes are easy to prepare.

Tofu is another widely used ingredient in Asian cookery. Made from the pressed curd of the soya bean, tofu is low in fat and rich in protein, making it perfect for vegetarians. It can be prepared in dozens of ways: boiled, stir-fried or deep-fried are just three methods described in this chapter for you to try.

SPICED OKRA WITH ALMONDS

Long and elegantly shaped, it's not surprising these vegetables are commonly called "lady's fingers". Native to tropical Africa, they are very popular in India and Arab countries.

INGREDIENTS

*50g/2oz/½ cup blanched
almonds, chopped
25g/1oz/2 tbsp butter
225g/8oz okra
15ml/1 tbsp sunflower oil
2 garlic cloves, crushed
2.5cm/1in piece fresh root ginger, grated
5ml/1 tsp cumin seeds
5ml/1 tsp ground coriander
5ml/1 tsp paprika
300ml/½ pint/1¼ cups water
salt and ground black pepper*

SERVES 2–4

1 In a shallow flameproof dish, fry the almonds in the butter until they are lightly golden. Remove from the pan with a slotted spoon and drain on kitchen paper.

2 Using a sharp knife, trim the tops of the okra stems and around the edges of the stalks. The pods contain a sticky liquid which oozes out if they are prepared too far in advance, so trim them just before cooking. Heat the oil in the pan, add the okra and fry, stirring constantly with a wooden spoon, for 2 minutes, until the okra starts to soften.

3 Add the garlic and ginger, and fry gently for 1 minute, then add the cumin seeds, coriander and paprika and cook for another 1–2 minutes, stirring all the time.

4 Pour in the measured water. Season generously with salt and pepper, cover the pan and simmer for about 5 minutes until the okra feels just tender when pierced with the tip of a sharp knife. Stir the mixture occasionally.

5 Finally, stir in the fried almonds and serve the dish piping hot.

SPICED AUBERGINES

The exact origins of the aubergine are uncertain but it has been cultivated in India since ancient times. It comes from the same family as the potato and is related to both the petunia and the tobacco plant.

INGREDIENTS
2 aubergines, halved lengthways
salt
60ml/4 tbsp olive oil, plus extra if needed
2 large onions, thinly sliced
2 garlic cloves, crushed
1 green pepper, seeded and sliced
400g/14oz can chopped tomatoes
40g/1½oz/3 tbsp sugar
5ml/1 tsp ground coriander
ground black pepper
30ml/2 tbsp chopped fresh coriander or parsley
fresh coriander sprigs, to garnish
crusty bread, to serve

SERVES 4

1 Using a sharp knife, slash the flesh of the aubergines a few times. Sprinkle with salt and drain in a colander for about 30 minutes. Rinse well and pat dry.

2 Gently fry the aubergines, cut-side down, in the oil for 5 minutes, then drain and place in a shallow ovenproof dish.

3 In the same pan, gently fry the onions, garlic and green pepper, adding extra oil if necessary. Cook for about 10 minutes, stirring occasionally, until all the vegetables have softened.

4 Add the tomatoes, sugar, ground coriander and black pepper to the onion and green pepper mixture. Stir to combine thoroughly, then cook for about 5 minutes until the mixture is reduced. Stir in the chopped coriander or parsley.

5 Preheat the oven to 190°C/375°F/Gas 5. Spoon the mixture on top of the halved aubergines, cover and bake for 30–35 minutes. Cool, garnish with coriander sprigs, and serve cold with crusty bread.

COOK'S TIP
Sprinkling the cut surfaces of aubergines with salt allows the juices that form to drain away in a colander. Before cooking, it is important to rinse the aubergines well and pat dry with kitchen paper. Prepared like this, aubergines are less bitter.

SPICED SPINACH AND POTATOES

I ndia has more than 18 varieties of spinach. If you have access to an Indian or Chinese supermarket, it is well worth looking out for some of the more unusual varieties.

INGREDIENTS
450g/1lb potatoes
60ml/4 tbsp vegetable oil
2.5cm/1in piece fresh root ginger, grated
4 garlic cloves, crushed
1 onion, coarsely chopped
2 green chillies, chopped
2 whole dried red chillies,
coarsely broken
5ml/1 tsp cumin seeds
225g/8oz fresh spinach, chopped or
225g/8oz frozen spinach, thawed and
drained
salt
2 firm tomatoes, peeled and coarsely
chopped, to garnish

SERVES 4–6

1 Cut large potatoes into quarters or, if using small new potatoes, leave them whole. Heat the oil in a frying pan and fry the potatoes until brown on all sides. Remove from the pan and set aside.

2 Pour off the excess oil from the pan, leaving 15ml/1 tbsp. Add the ginger, garlic, onion, green and red chillies and cumin seeds and fry gently until the onion is golden brown.

3 Add the potatoes, season with salt, and stir well. Cook, covered, until the potatoes are tender when pierced with the point of a sharp knife.

4 Add the spinach and stir well to mix with the potatoes. Cook, uncovered, until the spinach is tender and all the excess liquid has evaporated. Garnish with the chopped tomatoes and serve hot.

SPICY CABBAGE

An excellent accompaniment, this cabbage dish is very versatile and can even be served as a warm side salad or cold with a selection of cold meats. Try red cabbage for a change.

INGREDIENTS

50g/2oz/4 tbsp margarine or butter
2.5ml/½ tsp white cumin seeds
3–8 dried red chillies, to taste
1 small onion, sliced
225g/8oz/2½ cups shredded cabbage
2 carrots, grated
2.5ml/½ tsp salt
30ml/2 tbsp lemon juice

SERVES 4

3 Finally, stir in the salt and lemon juice. Taste for seasoning, then transfer to a warmed serving dish and serve immediately.

1 Put the margarine or butter into a saucepan and heat until melted. Add the cumin seeds. Crumble in the dried chillies and fry, stirring, for about 30 seconds.

2 Add the onion to the pan and fry for about 2 minutes. Add the cabbage and carrots and stir-fry for a further 5 minutes, or until the cabbage is soft.

KARAHI SHREDDED CABBAGE WITH CUMIN

T his cabbage dish is only lightly spiced and makes a good accompaniment to most other Balti and western dishes.

INGREDIENTS
15ml/1 tbsp corn oil
50g/2oz/4 tbsp butter
2.5ml/½ tsp crushed coriander seeds
2.5ml/½ tsp white cumin seeds
6 dried red chillies
1 small Savoy cabbage, shredded
12 mange-touts
12 baby sweetcorn
3 fresh red chillies, seeded and sliced
salt, to taste
*25g/1oz/¼ cup flaked almonds, toasted
and 15ml/1 tbsp chopped fresh
coriander, to garnish*

SERVES 4

1 Heat the oil with the butter in a deep round-bottomed frying pan or a karahi. When it is hot, add the crushed coriander seeds, white cumin seeds and dried red chillies and stir-fry for 1 minute.

2 Add the shredded cabbage and mange-touts and stir-fry for about 5 minutes.

3 Add the baby sweetcorn, chillies *(right)*, and salt and fry for 3 minutes, until the vegetables are tender.

4 Garnish with the toasted almonds and fresh coriander, and serve hot.

CAULIFLOWER WITH COCONUT

I n this dish, the creamy coconut sauce is the perfect contrast to the spiced cauliflower. Serve as a side-dish to traditional Indian dishes.

INGREDIENTS
15ml/1 tbsp plain flour
120ml/4fl oz/½ cup water
5ml/1 tsp chilli powder
15ml/1 tbsp ground coriander
5ml/1 tsp ground cumin
5ml/1 tsp mustard powder
5ml/1 tsp ground turmeric
60ml/4 tbsp vegetable oil
6–8 curry leaves
5ml/1 tsp cumin seeds
1 cauliflower, broken into florets
175ml/6fl oz/¾ cup thick coconut milk
juice of 2 lemons
salt
lime wedges, to garnish

SERVES 4–6

1 Mix the flour with a little of the water to make a smooth paste. Add the chilli, coriander, cumin, mustard, turmeric and salt to taste. Add the remaining water and keep mixing to blend all the ingredients well.

2 Heat the oil in a frying pan and fry the curry leaves and cumin seeds. Add the spice paste and simmer for about 5 minutes. If the sauce has become too thick, add a little hot water.

3 Add the cauliflower and coconut milk. Bring to the boil, cover and simmer until the cauliflower is tender but crunchy. Add the lemon juice, mix well, and serve hot garnished with lime wedges.

MIXED VEGETABLES IN COCONUT MILK

 most delicious way of cooking vegetables. If you don't like highly spiced food, use fewer red chillies.

INGREDIENTS
450g/1lb mixed vegetables, such as
aubergines, baby sweetcorn, carrots,
snake beans and patty pan squash
8 red chillies, seeded
2 lemon grass stalks, chopped
4 kaffir lime leaves, torn
30ml/2 tbsp vegetable oil
250ml/8fl oz/1 cup coconut milk
30ml/2 tbsp fish sauce
salt
15–20 Thai basil leaves, to garnish

SERVES 4–6

2 Put the red chillies, lemon grass and kaffir lime leaves in a mortar and grind together with a pestle.

3 Heat the oil in a wok or large deep frying pan. Add the chilli mixture and fry for 2–3 minutes.

4 Stir in the coconut milk and bring to the boil. Add the vegetables and cook for about 5 minutes or until they are tender. Season with the fish sauce and salt, and garnish with Thai basil leaves.

1 Cut the vegetables into similar-size shapes using a sharp knife.

BAMBOO SHOOT SALAD

This salad, which has a hot and sharp flavour, originated in north-east Thailand. Use fresh, young bamboo shoots when you can find them, otherwise substitute canned bamboo shoots.

INGREDIENTS

400g/14oz can whole bamboo shoots
25g/1oz glutinous rice
30ml/2 tbsp chopped shallots
15ml/1 tbsp chopped garlic
45ml/3 tbsp chopped spring onions
30ml/2 tbsp fish sauce
30ml/2 tbsp lime juice
5ml/1 tsp granulated sugar
2.5ml/½ tsp dried flaked chillies
20–25 small mint leaves
15ml/1 tbsp toasted sesame seeds

SERVES 4

1 Rinse and drain the bamboo shoots, finely slice and set aside.

2 Dry-roast the rice in a frying pan until it is golden brown. Remove and grind to fine crumbs with a pestle and mortar.

3 Tip the rice into a bowl, add the shallots, garlic, spring onions, fish sauce, lime juice, granulated sugar, chillies and half the mint leaves.

4 Mix thoroughly, then pour over the bamboo shoots and toss together. Serve sprinkled with sesame seeds and the remaining mint leaves.

TOFU AND GREEN BEAN RED CURRY

This is another curry that is simple and quick to make. This recipe uses green beans, but you can use almost any kind of vegetable, such as aubergines, bamboo shoots or broccoli.

INGREDIENTS

600ml/1 pint/2½ cups coconut milk
15ml/1 tbsp red curry paste
45ml/3 tbsp fish sauce
10ml/2 tsp palm sugar
225g/8oz button mushrooms
115g/4oz green beans, trimmed
175g/6oz tofu, rinsed and cut into
2cm/¾in cubes
4 kaffir lime leaves, torn
2 red chillies, sliced
coriander leaves, to garnish

SERVES 4–6

1 Put about one-third of the coconut milk in a wok or saucepan. Cook until it starts to separate and an oily sheen appears.

2 Add the red curry paste, fish sauce and sugar to the coconut milk. Mix together.

3 Add the mushrooms to the curry sauce. Stir and cook for 1 minute.

4 Stir in the rest of the coconut milk and bring back to the boil.

5 Add the green beans and tofu and simmer gently for another 4–5 minutes.

6 Stir in the torn kaffir lime leaves and sliced chillies. Serve garnished with the coriander leaves.

TOFU STIR-FRY

Tofu has a pleasant creamy texture, which makes a good contrast with crunchy stir-fried vegetables. It is favoured by vegetarians as it is an excellent meat substitute, high in protein and low in fat. Make sure you buy firm tofu, which cuts easily.

INGREDIENTS

115g/4oz hard white cabbage
2 green chillies
225g/8oz firm tofu
45ml/3 tbsp vegetable oil
2 cloves garlic, crushed
3 spring onions, chopped
175g/6oz French beans, topped and tailed
175g/6oz baby sweetcorn, halved
115g/4oz beansprouts
45ml/3 tbsp smooth peanut butter
25ml/1½ tbsp dark soy sauce
300ml/½ pint/1¼ cups coconut milk

SERVES 2–4

1 Shred the white cabbage thinly and set aside. Carefully remove the seeds from the chillies, chop the flesh finely and set aside. Cut the tofu into thin strips about 1cm/½in thick.

2 Heat the wok, then add 30ml/2 tbsp of the oil. When the oil is hot, add the bean curd, stir-fry for 3 minutes and remove. Set aside. Wipe out the wok with kitchen paper.

3 Add the remaining oil. When it is hot, add the garlic, cabbage, spring onions and chillies and stir-fry for 1 minute. Add the French beans, sweetcorn and bean-sprouts and stir-fry for a further 2 minutes.

4 Add the peanut butter and soy sauce. Stir well to coat the vegetables. Add the tofu to the vegetables.

5 Pour the coconut milk over the vegetables, simmer for 3 minutes and serve immediately.

CABBAGE SALAD

Asimple and delicious way of using cabbage. Other vegetables such as broccoli, calabrese, cauliflower and Chinese cabbage can also be used.

INGREDIENTS

30ml/2 tbsp fish sauce
grated rind of 1 lime
30ml/2 tbsp lime juice
120ml/4fl oz/½ cup coconut milk
30ml/2 tbsp vegetable oil
2 large red chillies, seeded and
cut into fine strips
6 garlic cloves, finely sliced
6 shallots, finely sliced
1 small cabbage, shredded
30ml/2 tbsp coarsely chopped roasted
peanuts, to serve

SERVES 4–6

1 Make the dressing by combining the fish sauce, lime rind and juice and coconut milk. Set aside.

2 Heat the oil in a wok or frying pan. Stir-fry the chillies, garlic and shallots, until the shallots are brown and crisp. Remove and set aside.

3 Blanch the cabbage in boiling salted water for about 2–3 minutes, drain and put into a bowl.

4 Stir the dressing into the cabbage, toss and mix well. Transfer the salad into a serving dish. Sprinkle with the fried shallot mixture and the chopped roasted peanuts.

STIR-FRIED MIXED VEGETABLES

When selecting different items for a dish, never mix ingredients indiscriminately. In their cooking, as in all things, the Chinese aim to achieve a harmonious balance of colour and texture.

INGREDIENTS
225g/8oz Chinese cabbage
115g/4oz baby sweetcorn
115g/4oz broccoli
1 large or 2 small carrots
60ml/4 tbsp vegetable oil
5ml/1 tsp salt
5ml/1 tsp light brown sugar
chicken stock or water, if necessary
15ml/1 tbsp light soy sauce
few drops of sesame oil (optional)

SERVES 4

1 Cut the Chinese cabbage into thick slices. Cut the sweetcorn lengthways, if wished. Separate the broccoli into florets and slice the carrots diagonally.

2 Heat the oil in a wok, add the Chinese cabbage, sweetcorn, broccoli and carrots and stir-fry for about 2 minutes.

3 Add the salt and sugar, and a little stock or water, if necessary, so the vegetables do not dry out, and continue stirring for another minute (*left*). Add the soy sauce and sesame oil, if using. Blend well into the vegetable mixture and serve immediately.

FRUIT AND RAW VEGETABLE GADO-GADO

 his tangy, fresh salad is ideal before a spicy main course, or to accompany a creamy curry.

INGREDIENTS
2 unripe pears, peeled at the last moment
1–2 eating apples
juice of ½ lemon
1 small, crisp lettuce or a banana leaf
½ cucumber, seeded, sliced and salted, set aside for 15 minutes, then rinsed and drained
6 small tomatoes, cut into wedges
3 slices fresh pineapple, cored and cut into wedges
3 eggs or 12 quail's eggs, hard-boiled and shelled
175g/6oz egg noodles, cooked, cooled and chopped
deep-fried onions, to garnish

FOR THE PEANUT SAUCE
15ml/1 tbsp tamarind pulp
2–4 fresh red chillies, seeded and ground
300ml/½ pint/1¼ cups coconut milk
350g/12oz crunchy peanut butter
15ml/1 tbsp dark soy sauce
salt
coarsely crushed peanuts, to garnish

SERVES 6

1 To make the peanut sauce, soak the tamarind pulp in 45ml/3 tbsp warm water, strain and reserve the juice. Put the chillies and coconut milk in a saucepan. Add the peanut butter and heat gently, stirring, until smooth.

2 Allow to simmer gently until the sauce thickens, then add the soy sauce and the tamarind juice. Season with salt to taste. Pour into a bowl and garnish with a few coarsely crushed peanuts.

3 To make the salad, peel and core the pears and apples, slice them and sprinkle the apples with lemon juice. Shred the lettuce leaves to form a bed for the salad in a shallow bowl or flat platter. Alternatively line with the whole banana leaf. Arrange the fruit and vegetables attractively on top.

4 Add the sliced or quartered hard-boiled eggs (leave quail's eggs whole) and the chopped noodles. Garnish with the deep-fried onions.

5 Serve at once, accompanied with a bowl of the peanut sauce.

COOK'S TIP
Any fruit or vegetable can be substituted for the ones mentioned here. Experiment with soft, sweet tropical fruits such as mango or lychees, combined with sharp fruits such as grapefruit or lemon, for extra zing, and an authentic sweet and sour experience.

PAK CHOI AND MUSHROOM STIR-FRY

T ry to buy all the types of mushrooms, if you can, as the variety of flavours gives great subtlety to the finished dish; the oyster and shiitake mushrooms have particularly distinctive flavours.

INGREDIENTS
4 dried black Chinese mushrooms
450g/1lb pak choi
50g/2oz oyster mushrooms
50g/2oz shiitake mushrooms
15ml/1 tbsp vegetable oil
1 garlic clove, crushed
30ml/2 tbsp oyster sauce

SERVES 4

COOK'S TIP
Pak choi is a type of cabbage with long thin stems and dark green leaves. Bok choy can be used instead. The leaves are crisper but the flavour is very similar.

1 Put the dried black Chinese mushrooms into a small bowl and pour over 150ml/¼ pint/⅔ cup boiling water. Leave for about 15 minutes to let them soften.

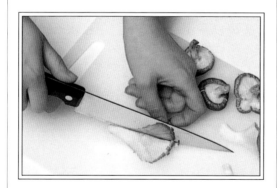

2 Meanwhile, tear the pak choi into bite-size pieces with your fingers. Using a sharp knife, halve any large oyster or shiitake mushrooms, using a sharp knife.

---

3 Strain the Chinese mushrooms. Heat the wok, then add the oil. When hot, stir-fry the garlic until softened but not coloured.

4 Add the pak choi and stir-fry for about 1 minute. Mix in all the mushrooms and stir-fry for 1 minute. Finally, add the oyster sauce, toss well and serve immediately.

VARIATION
Braise the mushrooms in a well-flavoured sauce. Omit the pak choi. Heat 15ml/1 tbsp oil in a wok, add a selection of mushrooms and stir-fry for 1 minute, then add 30ml/2 tbsp each of dark soy sauce, Chinese rice wine or dry sherry and sugar, 5ml/1 tsp sesame oil and 300ml/½ pint/1¼ cups chicken or vegetable stock. Reduce the heat and braise, stirring for 5–7 minutes until the liquid has almost evaporated.

STIR-FRIED BRUSSELS SPROUTS

An interesting way to cook Brussels sprouts, this method works equally well with shredded green cabbage. It is a recipe which also goes very well with European meals.

INGREDIENTS
450g/1lb Brussels sprouts, shredded
5ml/1 tsp sesame or sunflower oil
2 spring onions, sliced
2.5ml/½ tsp five-spice powder
15ml/1 tbsp light soy sauce
sliced spring onions, to garnish

SERVES 4

1 Trim the Brussels sprouts and remove any loose or yellowing leaves, then shred them finely, either using a large sharp knife or in a food processor.

2 Heat a wok or frying pan and then add the oil. When it is hot, add the Brussels sprouts and spring onions, and stir-fry for about 2 minutes, without letting the vegetables brown.

3 Stir in the five-spice powder and soy sauce (*left*), then cook, stirring, for a further 2–3 minutes, until just tender. Serve at once, garnished with the sliced spring onions.

CRISPY SEAWEED

I n northern China they use a special kind of seaweed for this dish, but spring greens, shredded very finely, make a very good alternative. Serve either as a starter or as a side dish.

INGREDIENTS
225g/8oz spring greens
groundnut or corn oil, for deep frying
1.5ml/¼ tsp salt
10ml/2 tsp soft light brown sugar
30–45ml/2–3 tbsp flaked toasted almonds,
to garnish

SERVES 4

1 Cut out and discard any tough stalks from the spring greens. Place about six leaves on top of each other and roll up tightly. Using a sharp knife, slice across into very thin shreds. Lay on a tray and leave to dry for about 2 hours.

2 Heat about 5–7.5cm/2–3in of oil in a heavy saucepan or wok to 190°C/375°F. Carefully place a handful of the leaves in the oil – it will bubble and spit for about the first 10 seconds and then die down. Deep-fry the leaves for about 45 seconds, or until they are a slightly darker green – do not let the leaves burn.

3 Remove the leaves with a slotted spoon, drain on kitchen paper and transfer to a serving dish. Keep warm in the oven while frying the remainder.

4 When you have deep-fried all the shredded leaves, sprinkle them with the salt and sugar and toss lightly so that they are all thoroughly coated. Garnish with the toasted almonds and serve immediately.

COOK'S TIP
Make sure that your pan is deep enough to allow the oil to bubble up during cooking. The pan should be less than half full.

TOFU AND CRUNCHY VEGETABLES

Tofu is best if it is marinated lightly before cooking to add extra flavour. Using smoked tofu makes this Chinese dish even tastier.

INGREDIENTS
2 × 225g/8oz cartons smoked tofu, cubed
45ml/3 tbsp soy sauce
30ml/2 tbsp dry sherry or vermouth
15ml/1 tbsp sesame oil
45ml/3 tbsp groundnut or sunflower oil
2 leeks, thinly sliced
2 carrots, cut into sticks
1 large courgette, thinly sliced
115g/4oz baby sweetcorn, halved
115g/4oz button or shiitake
mushrooms, sliced
15ml/1 tbsp sesame seeds
egg noodles, to serve

SERVES 4

COOK'S TIP
The secret of successful stir-frying is to have all your ingredients ready prepared before you heat the oil in the wok. Arrange vegetables on separate dishes and measure out sauces, oils and spices.

1 Place the tofu cubes in a large bowl and add the soy sauce, sherry or vermouth and the sesame oil. Stir to mix thoroughly, then cover and leave to marinate in a cool place for at least 30 minutes. Lift the tofu cubes out of the marinade with a slotted spoon, reserving the marinade.

2 Heat the groundnut or sunflower oil in a wok or large frying pan, add the tofu cubes and stir-fry until browned all over. Remove with a slotted spoon and set aside.

3 Stir-fry the leeks, carrots, courgette and baby sweetcorn, stirring and tossing for about 2 minutes. Add the mushrooms and stir-fry for 1 further minute.

4 Return the tofu cubes to the wok and pour in the reserved marinade. Heat until bubbling, then scatter over the sesame seeds. Serve immediately, straight from the wok, with hot noodles tossed in a little sesame oil if liked.

BRAISED VEGETABLES

T he original recipe calls for no fewer than 18 different ingredients to represent the 18 Buddhas. Later, this was reduced to eight, but nowadays anything between four and six items is regarded as more than sufficient.

INGREDIENTS

10g/¼oz dried wood-ear mushrooms
75g/3oz straw mushrooms, drained
75g/3oz sliced bamboo shoots, drained
50g/2oz mange-touts
225g/8oz tofu
175g/6oz Chinese cabbage
45–60ml/3–4 tbsp vegetable oil
5ml/1 tsp salt
2.5ml/½ tsp light brown sugar
15ml/1 tbsp light soy sauce
few drops of sesame oil (optional)

SERVES 4

1 Soak the wood-ear mushrooms in cold water for 20–25 minutes, then rinse and discard the hard stalks, if any. Cut the straw mushrooms in half lengthways; if large cut in pieces, if small keep them whole. Rinse and drain the bamboo shoot slices. Top and tail the mange-touts. Cut the tofu into about 12 small pieces. Cut the cabbage into pieces about the same size as the mange-touts.

2 Harden the tofu pieces by placing them in a saucepan of boiling water for about 2 minutes. Remove and drain.

3 Heat the oil in a wok or frying pan. When it is hot, add the tofu pieces and lightly brown on all sides. Remove with a slotted spoon and keep warm.

4 Add the wood-ear and straw mushrooms, bamboo shoots, mange-touts and Chinese cabbage to the wok or frying pan and stir-fry for about 1½ minutes, then add the tofu pieces, salt, sugar and soy sauce. Continue stirring for 1 further minute, then cover and braise for 2–3 minutes. Sprinkle with sesame oil, if using, transfer to a warmed platter and serve.

COOK'S TIP
When using dried mushrooms, first rinse them under cold running water to remove any grit, then soak in a bowl with water to cover by 5cm/2in.

FRENCH BEANS WITH SESAME SEEDS

his excellent Japanese dish is flavoured with a delicious Gomaae sauce made predominantly from sesame seeds. Serve it with other vegetables, such as spinach, if you like.

INGREDIENTS
200g/7oz French beans
salt

FOR THE GOMAAE SAUCE
60ml/4 tbsp white sesame seeds
10ml/2 tsp sugar
15ml/1 tbsp soy sauce
15ml/1 tbsp instant dashi

SERVES 4

1 Top and tail the French beans and then cook them in boiling salted water for about 2 minutes, or until they are tender.

2 Drain the cooked beans and soak them in cold water for 1 minute to preserve their colour. Drain well and cut into lengths of 3–4cm/1¼–1½ in. Chill for 5 minutes.

3 To make the sauce, grind the white sesame seeds in a pestle and mortar, leaving some of the sesame seeds whole. Alternatively, roughly chop the sesame seeds on a chopping board with a knife.

4 Put the ground white sesame seeds into a small mixing bowl and carefully stir in the sugar. Then add the soy sauce and the instant dashi. Mix all the ingredients together well with a rubber spatula.

5 To serve, put the chilled French beans in a large mixing bowl, add the sauce and toss well. Transfer the beans to four small bowls, and serve immediately.

MIXED VEGETABLE SOUP

he main ingredient for this soup is crushed tofu, which is both nutritious and satisfying.

INGREDIENTS

150g/5oz fresh Japanese tofu
2 dried shiitake mushrooms
50g/2oz gobo
5ml/1 tsp rice vinegar
1/2 black or white konnyaku, 125g/4¹/₄oz
30ml/2 tbsp sesame oil
115g/4oz mooli, thinly sliced
50g/2oz carrot, thinly sliced
700ml/generous 1 pint/scant 3 cups kombu and bonito stock or instant dashi
pinch of salt
30ml/2 tbsp sake or dry white wine
7.5ml/1¹/₂ tsp mirin
45ml/3 tbsp white or red miso paste
dash of soy sauce
6 mangetouts, trimmed, boiled and thinly sliced, to garnish

SERVES 4

1 Crush the tofu by hand until it resembles a lumpy scrambled egg texture – do not crush it too finely.

2 Wrap the tofu in a dish cloth and put it in a strainer, then pour over plenty of boiling water. Leave the tofu to drain thoroughly for 10 minutes.

3 Soak the dried shiitake mushrooms in tepid water for 20 minutes, then drain them, reserving the soaking water for stock. Remove their stems, and cut the caps into four to six pieces.

4 Use a vegetable brush to scrub the skin off the gobo and slice it carefully into thin shavings. Soak the shavings for about 5 minutes in plenty of cold water with the vinegar added to remove any bitter taste. Drain well.

5 Put the konnyaku in a small saucepan and pour over just enough water to cover it. Bring to the boil over a moderate heat, then drain and allow to cool. Using your hands, tear the konnyaku into 2cm/³/₄in lumps. Do not use a knife as smooth cuts will prevent it from absorbing flavour.

6 Heat the sesame oil in a deep saucepan. Add all the shiitake mushrooms, gobo, mooli, carrot and konnyaku. Stir-fry for 1 minute, then add the tofu and stir well.

7 Pour in the stock and add the salt, sake or wine and mirin. Bring to the boil. Skim the broth and simmer for 5 minutes.

8 In a small bowl, dissolve the miso paste in a little of the soup, then return it to the pan. Simmer the soup for 10 minutes, until the vegetables are soft. Add the soy sauce, then remove from the heat. Serve immediately in four bowls, garnished with the mangetouts.

COOK'S TIP
Konnyaku is a special cake made from flour that is produced from a root vegetable called devil's tongue. It has a subtle slightly fishy flavour.

BOILED FRIED TOFU WITH HIJIKI SEAWEED

oiled dishes, known as *nimono,* are enjoyed throughout the year in Japanese homes.

INGREDIENTS
20g/³/₄oz dried hijiki seaweed
1 sheet Japanese fried tofu (aburage)
30g/1¹/₄oz carrot
30g/1¹/₄oz fresh shiitake mushrooms,
stems removed
15ml/1 tbsp oil
100ml/3¹/₂ fl oz/generous ¹/₃ cup
instant dashi
22.5ml/4¹/₂ tsp sake or dry white wine
15ml/1 tbsp mirin
22.5ml/4¹/₂ tsp soy sauce
22.5ml/4¹/₂ tsp sugar

SERVES 4

1 Wash the hijiki seaweed and soak it in cold water for 30 minutes. Drain well. Do not soak for any longer as it will lack flavour. During soaking, the hijiki will expand to about six times its dried volume.

2 Put the tofu in a strainer and rinse with hot water from a kettle to remove any excess oil. Shred it to 3cm/1¼in lengths. Shred the carrot and shiitake mushrooms into strips of about the same size.

3 Heat the oil in a large pan. Add the carrot, stir once, then add the shiitake mushrooms and stir-fry over a high heat for 1 minute. Add the hijiki, stir, then add the fried tofu and stir-fry for 1 minute.

4 Pour in the dashi, sake or wine, mirin and soy sauce. Stir in the sugar. Bring to the boil and reduce the heat, then simmer until all the soup has evaporated, stirring occasionally. Serve the tofu hot or cold, in four small bowls.

COOK'S TIP
Hijiki is a dried seaweed with a high fibre content. If Japanese fried tofu is not available, Chinese fried tofu may be used instead.

WINTER TOFU AND VEGETABLES

This Japanese dish is brought bubbling hot to the table with a pot of dip to accompany the freshly cooked tofu and vegetables.

INGREDIENTS
1 sheet kombu seaweed,
20 x 10cm/8 x 4in
600g/1lb 5oz Japanese silken tofu,
10 x 8 x 3cm/4 x 3¹/₄ x 1¹/₄in
2 leeks
4 shiitake mushrooms, cross cut in top
and stems removed
spring onions, to garnish

FOR THE DIP
200ml/7fl oz/scant 1 cup soy sauce
generous 15ml/1 tbsp mirin
100ml/3¹/₂fl oz/generous ¹/₃ cup
bonito flakes

SERVES 4

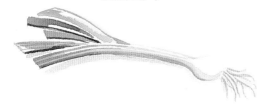

1 Half fill a large flameproof casserole or saucepan with cold water and soak the kombu seaweed in it for 30 minutes.

2 Cut the silken tofu into 4cm/1½in cubes. Slice the leeks diagonally into 2cm/¾in thick slices.

3 To make the dip, bring the soy sauce and mirin to the boil, then add the bonito flakes. Remove from the heat and leave until all the flakes have sunk to the bottom of the pan, then strain the sauce and pour it into a small heatproof basin.

4 Stand the basin in the middle of the pan, placing it on an upturned saucer, if necessary, so that it is well above the level of the water. This keeps the dip hot. Bring the water to the boil.

5 Add the mushrooms and leeks to the pan, and cook for about 5 minutes over a moderate heat until softened. Then gently add the tofu. When the tofu starts floating, it is ready to eat. If the tofu won't all fit in the pan, it can be added during the meal.

6 Take the pan to the table and spoon the dip into four small bowls. Sprinkle the spring onions into the dip. Diners help themselves to tofu and vegetables from the pan and eat them with the dip. The kombu seaweed is used only to flavour the dish; it is not eaten.

DEEP-FRIED TOFU AND ASPARAGUS IN STOCK

Agedashi is the name for dishes of deep-fried *(age)* ingredients served in a stock *(dashi)* or thin sauce. Here, deep-fried tofu and asparagus are served in a thin stock-based sauce and topped with tomato. A cup of sake goes very well with this *Agedashi*.

INGREDIENTS
200g/7oz fresh Japanese tofu,
10 x 5 x 3cm/4 x 2 x 1¼in
4 asparagus spears, trimmed of tough
stalk ends
1 beef tomato, skinned
oil, for deep frying
cornflour, for coating

FOR THE SAUCE
200ml/7fl oz/scant 1 cup instant dashi
50ml/2fl oz/¼ cup mirin
50ml/2fl oz/¼ cup soy sauce

SERVES 4

1 Wrap the tofu in a kitchen towel and press between two plates for 30 minutes, removing any excess moisture. Alternatively, wrap the tofu in kitchen paper, place it on a plate and cook it in the microwave for 1 minute (600W). Cut the tofu into eight cubes, each measuring about 2.5cm/1in.

2 Cut the asparagus into 3–4cm/1¼–1½in lengths. Halve the tomato and remove the seeds, then cut it into 5mm/¼in cubes.

3 Slowly heat the oil for deep frying to a temperature of 170°C/340°F. Coat the tofu with cornflour.

4 Deep fry the tofu pieces in two batches over a medium heat until golden, allowing 7–10 minutes to ensure that the tofu is cooked thoroughly. It starts to expand once it is cooked. Drain well. Keep the oil temperature at 170°C/340°F during cooking.

5 Meanwhile, place the ingredients for the sauce in a saucepan and bring to the boil, then simmer gently for 3 minutes. Deep fry the asparagus lengths for 2 minutes and drain them well.

6 Place the tofu on a large plate and arrange the asparagus on top. Pour on the hot sauce and sprinkle the tomato on

PINEAPPLE FRIED RICE

W hen buying a pineapple, look for a sweet-smelling fruit with an even brownish/yellow skin. To test for ripeness, tap the base – a dull sound indicates that the fruit is ripe. The flesh should also give slightly when pressed.

INGREDIENTS
1 pineapple
30ml/2 tbsp vegetable oil
1 small onion, finely chopped
2 green chillies, seeded and chopped
225g/8oz lean pork,
cut into small dice
115g/4oz cooked shelled prawns
675–900g/1½–2 lb/3–4 cups
cold cooked rice
50g/2oz roasted cashew nuts
2 spring onions, chopped
30ml/2 tbsp fish sauce
15ml/1 tbsp soy sauce
2 red chillies and 1 green chilli, sliced,
and 10–12 mint leaves, to garnish

SERVES 4–6

1 Cut the pineapple in half lengthways and remove the flesh from both halves by cutting round inside the skin. Reserve the skin shells. You need 115g/4oz of fruit, chopped finely (keep the rest for a dessert).

2 Heat the oil in a wok or large frying pan. Add the onion and chillies and fry for about 3–5 minutes until softened. Add the pork and cook until it is brown on all sides.

3 Stir in the prawns and rice and toss well together. Continue to stir-fry until the rice is thoroughly heated. Add the chopped pineapple, cashew nuts and spring onions. Season with fish sauce and soy sauce.

4 Spoon into the pineapple skin shells. Garnish with red and green chillies and shredded mint leaves.

COOK'S TIP
This dish is ideal to prepare for a special-occasion meal. Served in the pineapple skin shells, it is sure to be the talking point of the dinner.

189

THAI FRIED NOODLES

P hat Thai has a fascinating flavour and texture. It is made with rice noodles and is considered one of the national dishes of Thailand.

INGREDIENTS

350g/12oz rice noodles
45ml/3 tbsp vegetable oil
15ml/1 tbsp chopped garlic
16 uncooked king prawns, shelled, tails left intact and de-veined
2 eggs, lightly beaten
15ml/1 tbsp dried shrimps, rinsed
30ml/2 tbsp pickled white radish
50g/2oz fried tofu, cut into small slivers
2.5ml/1/2 tsp dried chilli flakes
115g/4oz garlic chives, cut into 5cm/2in lengths
225g/8oz beansprouts
50g/2oz roasted peanuts, coarsely ground
5ml/1 tsp granulated sugar
15ml/1 tbsp dark soy sauce
30ml/2 tbsp fish sauce
30ml/2 tbsp tamarind juice
30ml/2 tbsp coriander leaves and 1 kaffir lime cut into wedges, to garnish

SERVES 4–6

1 Soak the noodles in warm water for 20–30 minutes, then drain.

2 Heat 15ml/1 tbsp of the oil in a wok or large frying pan. Add the garlic and fry until golden. Stir in the prawns and cook for about 1–2 minutes until pink, tossing from time to time. Remove and set aside.

3 Heat another 15ml/1 tbsp of oil in the wok. Add the eggs and tilt the wok to spread them into a thin sheet. Stir to scramble and break the egg into small pieces. Remove from the wok and set aside with the prawns.

4 Heat the remaining oil in the same wok. Add the dried shrimps, pickled white radish, fried bean curd and dried chilli flakes. Stir briefly. Add the soaked noodles and stir-fry for 5 minutes.

5 Add the garlic chives, half the beansprouts and half the ground peanuts. Season with the granulated sugar, soy sauce, fish sauce and tamarind juice. Mix well and cook until the noodles are heated through.

6 Return the prawn and egg mixture to the wok and mix with the noodles. Serve garnished with the rest of the beansprouts, peanuts, coriander leaves and lime wedges.

CHIANG MAI NOODLE SOUP

A signature dish of the city of Chiang Mai, this delicious noodle soup has Burmese origins and is the Thai equivalent of the Malaysian "Laksa".

INGREDIENTS

600ml/1 pint/2½ cups coconut milk
30ml/2 tbsp red curry paste
5ml/1 tsp ground turmeric
450g/1lb chicken thighs, boned and cut into bite-size chunks
600ml/1 pint/2½ cups chicken stock
60ml/4 tbsp fish sauce
15ml/1 tbsp dark soy sauce
juice of ½–1 lime
450g/1lb fresh egg noodles, blanched briefly in boiling water
salt and freshly ground black pepper

FOR THE GARNISH

3 spring onions, chopped
4 red chillies, seeded and chopped
4 shallots, chopped
60ml/4 tbsp sliced pickled mustard leaves, rinsed
30ml/2 tbsp fried sliced garlic coriander leaves
4 fried noodle nests (optional)

SERVES 4–6

1 Put one third of the coconut milk into a large saucepan, bring to the boil and stir with a wooden spoon until it separates.

2 Add the curry paste and ground turmeric, stir to mix completely and cook until fragrant.

3 Add the chicken and stir-fry for about 2 minutes, ensuring that all the chunks are coated with the paste.

4 Add the remaining coconut milk, chicken stock, fish sauce and soy sauce. Season with salt and freshly ground black pepper to taste. Simmer gently for about 7–10 minutes. Remove from the heat and stir in the lime juice.

5 Reheat the noodles in boiling water, drain and divide between individual bowls. Divide the chicken between the bowls and ladle in the hot soup. Top each serving with a few of each of the garnishes.

INDONESIAN PORK AND PRAWN RICE

asi Goreng is one of the most familiar and well-loved Indonesian dishes. It is a marvellous way to use up leftover rice, chicken and other meats such as pork. It is important that the rice is cold and the grains are separated before adding the other ingredients, so it is best to cook the rice the day before.

INGREDIENTS
350g/12oz/1½ cups long-grain rice, such
as basmati, cooked and left until cold
2 eggs
30ml/2 tbsp water
105ml/7 tbsp oil
225g/8oz pork fillet or fillet of beef
115g/4oz cooked, peeled prawns
175g–225g/6–8oz cooked
chicken, chopped
2–3 fresh red chillies, seeded and sliced
1cm/½in cube terasi
2 garlic cloves, crushed
1 onion, sliced
30ml/2 tbsp dark soy sauce or
45–60ml/3–4 tbsp tomato ketchup
salt and freshly ground black pepper
celery leaves, deep-fried onions and
coriander sprigs, to garnish

SERVES 4–6

1 Cook and cool the rice. Fork it through to separate the grains and keep it in a covered pan or dish until required.

2 Beat the eggs. Add the seasoning and water and make two or three omelettes in a frying pan, with a small amount of oil. Roll up each omelette, leave to cool, and cut in strips when cold. Set aside.

3 Cut the pork or beef into neat strips and put the meat, prawns and chicken pieces into separate bowls. Shred one of the chillies and reserve it.

4 Put the *terasi*, with the remaining chilli, garlic and onion in a food processor and grind to a fine paste. Alternatively, pound together using a pestle and mortar.

5 Fry the paste in the remaining hot oil, without browning, until it gives off a rich, spicy aroma, for about 3 minutes. Add the pork or beef, tossing the meat all the time, to seal in the juices. Cook for 2 minutes, stirring constantly.

6 Add the prawns, cook for a further 2 minutes, and then stir in the chicken, cold rice, dark soy sauce or ketchup and season to taste. Stir all the time to keep the rice light and fluffy and prevent it from sticking to the pan.

7 Turn the rice mixture on to a hot platter and garnish with the omelette strips, celery leaves, deep-fried onions, reserved shredded chilli and the fresh, chopped coriander sprigs.

EGG FRIED NOODLES

Yellow bean sauce gives these noodles a savoury flavour. They are eaten all over Asia, accompanying many meat and vegetable dishes.

INGREDIENTS
350g/12oz medium-thick egg noodles
60ml/4 tbsp vegetable oil
4 spring onions, cut into
1cm/½in rounds
juice of 1 lime
15ml/1 tbsp soy sauce
2 garlic cloves, finely chopped
175g/6oz skinless, boneless chicken breast, sliced
175g/6oz raw prawns, peeled and deveined
175g/6oz squid, cleaned and cut into rings
15ml/1 tbsp yellow bean sauce
15ml/1 tbsp fish sauce
15ml/1 tbsp soft light brown sugar
2 eggs
coriander leaves, to garnish

SERVES 4–6

1 Cook the noodles in a saucepan of boiling water until just tender, then drain well and set aside.

2 Heat half the oil in a wok or large frying pan. Add the spring onions, stir-fry for 2 minutes, then add the noodles, lime juice and soy sauce and stir-fry for a further 2–3 minutes. Transfer the mixture to a bowl, cover, and keep warm.

3 Heat the remaining oil in the wok or pan. Add the garlic, chicken, prawns and squid. Stir-fry over a high heat for about 5 minutes or until all the ingredients are cooked through.

4 Stir in the yellow bean sauce, fish sauce and sugar, then break the eggs into the mixture, one at a time, stirring gently until they set.

5 Add the noodles to the wok or pan. Mix all the ingredients together well, and heat through. Serve garnished with fresh coriander leaves.

SOFT FRIED NOODLES

This basic, traditional dish is an ideal accompaniment for rich or spicy main courses.

INGREDIENTS
300g/11oz dried egg noodles
30ml/2 tbsp vegetable oil
30ml/2 tbsp finely chopped spring onions
soy sauce, to taste
salt and freshly ground black pepper
chopped spring onion, to garnish
deep-fried onion rings, to serve

SERVES 4–6

1 Cook the noodles in a large saucepan of boiling water until just tender, following the directions on the packet. Drain, rinse under cold running water to remove any excess starch, and drain again thoroughly.

2 Heat the oil in a wok and swirl it around. Add the spring onions and fry for about 30 seconds. Add the noodles, stirring gently to separate the strands.

3 Reduce the heat and fry the noodles, until they are lightly browned and crisp on the outside, but still soft on the inside.

4 Season with soy sauce, salt and freshly ground black pepper. Garnish with chopped spring onions and serve at once with deep-fried onion rings.

SEAFOOD CHOW MEIN

Chow mein is a Chinese-American dish in which a combination of seafood, chicken and vegetables are cooked separately and then combined with stir-fried noodles. This basic recipe can be adapted according to taste, using different items for the "dressing".

INGREDIENTS

75g/3oz squid, cleaned
75g/3oz raw prawns
3–4 fresh scallops
½ egg white
15ml/1 tbsp cornflour, mixed with a little water
250g/9oz egg noodles
75–90ml/5–6 tbsp vegetable oil
50g/2oz mange-touts
2.5ml/½ tsp salt
2.5ml/½ tsp light brown sugar
15ml/1 tbsp Chinese rice wine or dry sherry
30ml/2 tbsp light soy sauce
2 spring onions, finely sliced
chicken stock, if necessary
few drops of sesame oil

SERVES 4

1 Open up the squid and score the inside in a criss-cross pattern. Cut the squid into 1–2.5cm/½–1in pieces and soak in boiling water until all the pieces curl up. Rinse in cold water and drain.

2 Peel the prawns and cut each in half lengthways. Cut each scallop into 3 thin slices. Mix the scallops and prawns with the egg white and cornflour paste.

3 Cook the noodles in boiling water according to the manufacturer's instructions, then drain and rinse under cold water. Mix with about 15ml/1 tbsp of the oil.

4 Heat about 15–30ml/2–3 tbsp of the oil in a wok until hot. Stir-fry the mange-touts and seafood for about 2 minutes, then add the salt, sugar, wine or sherry, half of the soy sauce and the sliced spring onions. Stir the mixture and add a little stock if necessary. Remove and keep warm.

5 Heat the remaining oil in the wok and stir-fry the noodles for 2–3 minutes with the remaining soy sauce. Place the noodles in a large serving dish and pour the seafood mixture over them. Sprinkle with a few drops of sesame oil. Either serve at once or, if you prefer, when cold.

SPECIAL CHOW MEIN

L ap cheong is a special air-dried Chinese sausage. It is available from most Chinese supermarkets. If you cannot buy it, substitute for diced ham, chorizo or salami.

INGREDIENTS
45ml/3 tbsp vegetable oil
2 garlic cloves, sliced
5ml/1 tsp chopped root ginger
2 red chillies, chopped
2 lap cheong, about 75g/3oz, rinsed and sliced (optional)
1 boneless chicken breast, thinly sliced
16 uncooked tiger prawns, shelled, tails left intact and deveined
115g/4oz green beans
225g/8oz beansprouts
50g/2oz garlic chives
450g/1lb egg noodles, cooked in boiling water until tender
30ml/2 tbsp soy sauce
15ml/1 tbsp oyster sauce
15ml/1 tbsp sesame oil
salt and freshly ground black pepper
2 spring onions, shredded, and
15ml/1 tbsp coriander leaves, to garnish

SERVES 4–6

1 Heat 15ml/1 tbsp of the oil in a wok or large frying pan and fry the garlic, ginger and chillies. Add the lap cheong (or its substitute), chicken, prawns and beans. Stir-fry for about 2 minutes over a high heat or until the chicken and prawns are cooked. Transfer the mixture to a bowl and set aside.

2 Heat the rest of the oil in the same wok. Add the beansprouts and garlic chives. Stir-fry for 1–2 minutes.

3 Add the noodles and toss and stir to mix. Season with soy sauce, oyster sauce, salt and pepper.

4 Return the prawn mixture to the wok. Reheat and mix well with the noodles. Stir in the sesame oil. Serve garnished with spring onions and coriander leaves.

NOODLES WITH VEGETABLES

This Chinese dish makes a delicious vegetarian supper on its own, or serve it as a side dish with a main course of fish, meat or poultry.

INGREDIENTS

225g/8oz egg noodles
15ml/1 tbsp sesame oil
45ml/3 tbsp groundnut oil
2 garlic cloves, thinly sliced
2.5cm/1in piece fresh root ginger,
finely chopped
2 fresh red chillies, seeded and sliced
115g/4oz broccoli, broken into
small florets
115g/4oz baby sweetcorn
175g/6oz shiitake or oyster
mushrooms, sliced
1 bunch spring onions, sliced
115g/4oz pak choi or Chinese
cabbage, shredded
115g/4oz beansprouts
15–30ml/1–2 tbsp dark soy sauce
salt and ground black pepper

SERVES 4

1 Cook the egg noodles in a pan of boiling salted water according to the manufacturer's instructions. Drain well and toss in the sesame oil. Set aside.

2 Heat the groundnut oil in a wok or large frying pan and stir-fry the garlic and ginger for 1 minute. Add the chillies, broccoli, baby sweetcorn and mushrooms and stir-fry for a further 2 minutes.

3 Add the sliced spring onions, shredded pak choi or cabbage and the beansprouts to the wok. Stir-fry for about 2 minutes.

4 Toss in the noodles, soy sauce and black pepper. Continue to cook over a high heat for 2–3 minutes, until the ingredients are well mixed and warmed through. Serve at once.

SWEET AND SOUR NOODLES

Noodles combined with chicken and a selection of vegetables in a tasty sweet and sour sauce create a quick and satisfying meal.

INGREDIENTS

275g/10oz egg noodles
30ml/2 tbsp vegetable oil
3 spring onions, chopped
1 garlic clove, crushed
2.5cm/1in piece fresh root ginger, peeled and grated
5ml/1 tsp hot paprika
5ml/1 tsp ground coriander
3 boneless chicken breasts, sliced
115g/4oz mange-touts, topped and tailed
115g/4oz baby sweetcorn
225g/8oz fresh beansprouts
15ml/1 tbsp cornflour
45ml/3 tbsp soy sauce
45ml/3 tbsp lemon juice
15ml/1 tbsp sugar
45ml/3 tbsp chopped fresh coriander or spring onion tops, to garnish

SERVES 4

1 Bring a large saucepan of salted water to the boil. Add the noodles and cook according to the manufacturer's instructions. Drain, cover and keep warm.

2 Heat the oil in a wok or large frying pan. Add the spring onions and cook over a gentle heat. Mix in the garlic, ginger, paprika, ground coriander and chicken, then stir-fry for 3–4 minutes. Add the mangetouts, baby sweetcorn and beansprouts and steam briefly. Then stir in the cooked noodles.

3 Combine the cornflour, soy sauce, lemon juice and sugar in a small bowl. Add to the wok and simmer briefly to thicken. Serve garnished with chopped coriander or spring onion tops.

MIXED RICE

Rice is a staple part of the Japanese diet and this is one of the many ways of cooking it. This recipe makes a very good party dish, and you can add a variety of ingredients to create your own special version. *Aburage*, a deep fried tofu, is sold ready-made in Japanese shops.

INGREDIENTS
6 dried shiitake mushrooms
2 sheets fried tofu (aburage)*, each*
13 x 6cm/5 x 2½in
6 mangetouts
1 carrot, cut into matchstick strips
115g/4oz chicken fillet, diced
30ml/2 tbsp sugar
37.5ml/7½ tsp soy sauce
salt
1kg/2¼lb/7 cups freshly boiled
Japanese rice

SERVES 4

1 Soak the dried shiitake mushrooms in 800ml/27fl oz/3½ cups water for about 30 minutes. Place a small plate or saucer on top of the mushrooms to keep them submerged during soaking.

2 Put the fried tofu into a strainer and pour over hot water from a kettle to remove any excess fat. Squeeze the tofu and cut it in half lengthways, then slice it into 5mm/¼in wide strips.

3 Boil the mangetouts, then drain and refresh them in cold water. Drain well. Shred the mangetouts finely.

4 Drain the shiitake mushrooms, reserving the soaking water, and carefully remove their stems. Using a sharp knife, finely slice the mushroom caps. Pour the soaking water into a saucepan and add the tofu, carrots, chicken and shiitake mushrooms.

5 Bring the ingredients to the boil, then skim the broth and simmer for about 1–2 minutes. Add the sugar and cook for 1 minute, then add the soy sauce and salt. Simmer gently until most of the liquid has evaporated, leaving only a small amount of concentrated broth.

6 Mix in the boiled hot rice, sprinkle the mangetouts over the top and serve the mixed rice at once.

CHILLED NOODLES

These classic Japanese cold noodles are known as *somen*. The noodles are surprisingly refreshing when eaten with the accompanying ingredients and a delicately flavoured dip. The noodles are served with ice to ensure that they remain chilled until they are eaten.

INGREDIENTS

oil, for cooking
2 small eggs, beaten with a pinch of salt
1 sheet yaki-nori *seaweed, finely shredded*
1/2 bunch of spring onions, sliced
20ml/4 tsp wasabi paste
400g/14oz dried somen *noodles*
ice cubes, to serve

FOR THE DIP

1 litre/1¾ pints/4 cups kombu and bonito
stock or instant dashi
200ml/7fl oz/scant 1 cup soy sauce
15ml/1 tbsp mirin

SERVES 4

1 Prepare the dip in advance so that it has time to cool and chill. Bring the ingredients to the boil, then leave to cool and chill thoroughly.

2 Heat a little oil in a frying pan. Pour in half the beaten eggs, tilting the pan to coat the base evenly. Leave the egg to set, then turn it over and cook the second side briefly. Turn the omelette out on to a board. Cook the remaining egg in the same way.

3 Leave the omelettes to cool and then shred them finely. Divide the shredded omelette, *yaki-nori*, spring onions and wasabi among four small bowls.

4 Boil the *somen* noodles according to the packet instructions and drain. Rinse the noodles in or under cold running water, stirring with chopsticks, then drain well.

5 Place the cooked noodles on a large plate and add some ice cubes on top to keep them cool.

6 Pour the cold dip into four more small bowls. The noodles and the selected accompaniments are dipped into the chilled dip before they are eaten.

FIVE-FLAVOUR NOODLES

he Japanese title for this dish is *Gomoku Yakisoba*, meaning five different ingredients.

INGREDIENTS
300g/11oz dried Chinese thin egg noodles or 500g/1¼lb fresh yakisoba *noodles*
200g/7oz lean boneless pork, thinly sliced
22.5ml/4½ tsp oil
10g/¼oz fresh root ginger, grated
1 garlic clove, crushed
200g/7oz/1¾ cups green cabbage, roughly chopped
115g/4oz/½ cup beansprouts
1 green pepper, seeded and cut into fine strips
1 red pepper, seeded and cut into fine strips
salt and white pepper
20ml/4 tsp ao-nori seaweed, to garnish (optional)

FOR THE SEASONING
60ml/4 tbsp Worcestershire sauce
15ml/1 tbsp soy sauce
15ml/1 tbsp oyster sauce
15ml/1 tbsp sugar
2.5ml/½ tsp salt

SERVES 4

1 Boil the noodles according to the packet instructions and drain. Cut the pork into 3–4cm/1¼–1½in strips and season with salt and white pepper.

2 Heat 7.5ml/1½ tsp oil in a large frying pan or a wok and stir-fry the pork until just cooked, then remove it from the pan.

3 Wipe the pan with kitchen paper, and then heat the remaining oil in it. Add the ginger, garlic and cabbage and stir-fry for 1 minute.

4 Add the beansprouts and stir until softened, then add the green and red peppers and stir-fry for 1 minute.

5 Replace the pork in the pan and add the noodles. Stir in all the seasoning ingredients and more white pepper if you like. Stir-fry for 2–3 minutes.

6 Serve immediately, sprinkled with the *ao-nori* seaweed, if liked.

INDIVIDUAL NOODLE CASSEROLES

Traditionally, these individual casseroles are cooked in separate earthenware pots. *Nabe* means pot and *yaki* means to heat, providing the Japanese title of *Nabeyaki Udon* for this exciting recipe.

INGREDIENTS
115g/4oz boneless chicken thigh
2.5ml/¹/₂ tsp salt
2.5ml/¹/₂ tsp sake or dry white wine
2.5ml/¹/₂ tsp soy sauce
1 leek
115g/4oz whole spinach, trimmed
300g/11oz dried udon noodles or
500g/1¹/₄lb fresh
4 shiitake mushrooms, stems removed
4 size 4 eggs
seven flavour spice, to serve (optional)

FOR THE SOUP
1.4 litres/2¹/₃ pints/6 cups instant dashi
22.5ml/4¹/₂ tsp soy sauce
7ml/1¹/₃ tsp salt
15ml/1 tbsp mirin

SERVES 4

1 Cut the chicken thigh into small chunks and sprinkle with the salt, sake or wine and soy sauce. Cut the leek diagonally into 1.5cm/1³/₄in slices.

2 Boil the spinach for 2 minutes. Drain and soak in cold water for 1 minute. Drain, squeeze and cut into 4cm/1¹/₂in lengths.

3 Boil the dried *udon* noodles according to the packet instructions, allowing 3 minutes less than the suggested cooking time. If using fresh *udon* noodles, place them in boiling water, disentangle the noodles well and then drain them.

> ### COOK'S TIP
> Always use hot rice to make these balls, then allow them to cool before wrapping each one in clear film.

4 Bring the ingredients for the soup to the boil in a saucepan and add the chicken and leeks. Skim the broth, then cook it for 5 minutes.

5 Divide the *udon* noodles among four individual flameproof casseroles. Pour the soup, chicken and leeks into the casseroles. Place over a moderate heat, then add the shiitake mushrooms.

6 Gently break an egg into each casserole. Cover and simmer for 2 minutes. Divide the spinach among the casseroles and simmer for 1 minute.

7 Serve immediately, standing the hot casseroles on plates or table mats. Sprinkle seven flavour spice over the casseroles, if liked.

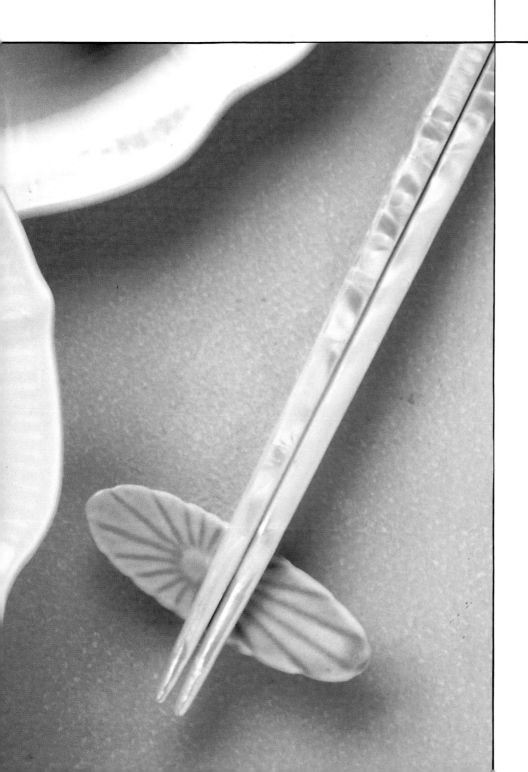

DESSERTS

After most Asian meals, dessert consists of
different types of fruit, simply prepared. In India
or Thailand, delicious mangoes may be prepared
in sorbets or ice creams. In China the ubiquitous
toffee apple is a popular dessert along with
lychees and pineapples.

Indians, however, are known for having a
sweet tooth and Kulfi, the frozen dessert made
from evaporated milk, nuts and rose-water, is a
favourite treat. Not surprisingly from countries
that eat so much rice and pasta, these
ingredients also figure highly in puddings, with
additions such as coconut milk in Thailand and
saffron and pistachios in India. Chinese desserts
feature sweetened red bean paste, used in
pancakes, along with some other very unusual
and delicious dishes, well worth trying.

KULFI

I n India *kulfi-wallahs* (ice cream vendors) have always made *kulfi*, and continue to this day, without using modern freezers. *Kulfi* is packed into metal cones sealed with dough and then churned in clay pots until set. This method works extremely well in an ordinary freezer.

INGREDIENTS
3 × 400ml/14fl oz cans evaporated milk
3 egg whites, whisked until peaks form
350g/12oz/2¼ cups icing sugar
5ml/1 tsp ground cardamom
15ml/1 tbsp rose-water
175g/6oz/1½ cups pistachios, chopped
75g/3oz/½ cup sultanas
75g/3oz/¾ cup flaked almonds
8 glacé cherries, halved

SERVES 4–6

1 Remove the labels from the cans of evaporated milk and lie the cans in one large, or two small heavy-based saucepans with tight-fitting lids. Fill the pan with water to reach three-quarters of the way up the cans. Bring to the boil, cover the pan, and simmer for about 20 minutes. When cool, remove from the pan and chill for 24 hours.

2 Open the cans and pour the evaporated milk into a large chilled bowl. Whisk until it doubles in volume, then fold in the whisked egg whites and the icing sugar.

3 Gently fold in the cardamom, rose-water, pistachios, sultanas, almonds and glacé cherries. Cover the bowl with clear film and leave in the freezer for 1 hour.

4 Remove the ice cream from the freezer and mix well with a fork to break up any ice crystals that have formed around the edge. Transfer to a freezer container and return to the freezer to freeze completely. Remove the ice cream from the freezer 10 minutes before serving to soften a little. Scoop into a chilled bowl to serve.

ORANGES WITH SAFFRON YOGURT

After a hot, spicy curry, a popular Indian pudding is simply sliced, juicy oranges sprinkled with a little cinnamon and served with a spoonful of saffron-flavoured yogurt.

INGREDIENTS
4 large oranges
1.5ml/¼ tsp ground cinnamon
150g/5oz/⅔ cup natural yogurt
10ml/2 tsp caster sugar
3–4 saffron strands
1.5ml/¼ tsp ground ginger
15ml/1 tbsp chopped pistachios, toasted
fresh lemon balm or mint
sprigs, to decorate

SERVES 4

1 Slice the bottoms off the oranges so they sit upright on a board. Working from the top of the oranges, cut across the top and down one side. Follow the contours of the orange to reveal the orange flesh beneath the pith. Repeat until all the rind and pith has been removed, reserving any juice.

COOK'S TIP
Instead of ordinary oranges, try using clementines or blood oranges.

2 Slice the oranges thinly and remove any pips. Place the oranges in a single layer, overlapping the slices, on a shallow serving platter. Sprinkle over the ground cinnamon, then cover and chill until you are ready to serve the dessert.

3 Mix together the yogurt, sugar, saffron and ginger in a bowl and leave to stand for 5 minutes. Spoon into a serving bowl and sprinkle with the nuts. Spoon a little of the yogurt mixture on to each serving and decorate with lemon balm or mint sprigs.

LASSI

L assi is a very popular drink both in India and Pakistan. It is available from both roadside cafes and good hotels. There is no substitute for this drink, especially on a hot day. It is ideal served with hot dishes, as it helps the body to digest spicy food.

INGREDIENTS
300ml/½ pint/1¼ cups natural yogurt
5ml/1 tsp sugar or to taste
300ml/½ pint/1¼ cups iced water
30ml/2 tbsp puréed fruit (optional)
15ml/1 tbsp crushed pistachio nuts

SERVES 4

COOK'S TIP
Fruit purée provides a filling, refreshing addition to traditional lassi. Try using strawberries, raspberries, mangoes and oranges – either fresh or frozen.

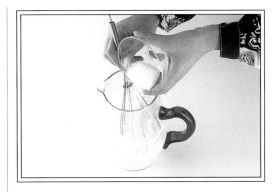

1 Place the yogurt in a jug and whisk it for about 2 minutes until frothy. Add the sugar to taste.

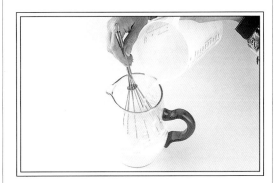

2 Pour in the water and the puréed fruit, if using, and continue to whisk for about 2 minutes.

3 Pour the lassi into tall serving glasses. Serve chilled, decorated with crushed pistachio nuts.

MANGO SORBET WITH MANGO SAUCE

After a spicy meal, this makes a most refreshing dessert. Mango is said to be one of the most ancient fruits cultivated in India, having been brought by the god Shiva for his wife, Parvati.

INGREDIENTS
900g/2lb mango pulp
2.5ml/½ tsp lemon juice
grated rind of 1 orange and 1 lime
4 egg whites, whisked until peaks form
50g/2oz/¼ cup caster sugar
120ml/4fl oz/½ cup double cream
50g/2oz/⅓ cup icing sugar

SERVES 4–6

COOK'S TIP
To prepare mango pulp, cut each mango lengthways on both sides of the stone, then slice the remaining mango from the stone. Make a lattice of cuts through each piece, cutting through the flesh but not the skin. Press the skin, so that the mango looks like a hedgehog, then cut the flesh from the skin. Purée in a blender.

1 In a large chilled bowl, mix 425g/15oz of the mango pulp with the lemon juice and the orange and lime rind.

2 Gently fold in the egg whites and caster sugar. Cover with clear film and place in the freezer for at least 1 hour.

3 Remove the mango mixture from the freezer and beat thoroughly. Transfer to a freezer and freeze fully.

4 To make the sauce, whip the double cream with the icing sugar and the remaining mango pulp. Cover and chill the sauce for 24 hours. Remove the sorbet from the freezer 10 minutes before serving so that it softens slightly. Using a spoon or ice cream scoop, transfer individual servings to chilled bowls and top each with a generous helping of mango sauce.

VERMICELLI PUDDING

I ndian vermicelli, made from wheat, has a much finer texture than the Italian variety. It is readily available from Asian shops as *seviyan*.

INGREDIENTS
115g/4oz fine vermicelli
1.2 litres/2 pints/5 cups water
2.5ml/½ tsp saffron strands
15ml/1 tbsp sugar
15ml/1 tbsp each shredded fresh coconut
or desiccated coconut, flaked almonds,
chopped pistachios and
sugar, to decorate
60ml/4 tbsp fromage
frais, to serve (optional)

SERVES 4

1 Crush the vermicelli in your hands and place in a saucepan. Pour in the water, add the saffron and bring to the boil. Boil for about 5 minutes.

2 Stir in the sugar and continue cooking until the water has evaporated from the vermicelli. Strain through a sieve, if necessary, to remove any excess liquid.

3 Ladle the vermicelli into a serving dish and decorate with the coconut, flaked almonds, chopped pistachios and sugar. Serve with fromage frais, if wished.

BAKED RICE PUDDING, THAI-STYLE

Black glutinous rice, also known as black sticky rice, has long black grains and a nutty taste similar to wild rice. This baked pudding has a distinct character and flavour all of its own.

INGREDIENTS
175g/6oz white or black glutinous (sticky) rice
30ml/2 tbsp soft light brown sugar
475ml/16fl oz/2 cups coconut milk
250ml/8fl oz/1 cup water
3 eggs
30ml/2 tbsp granulated sugar
icing sugar, to decorate

SERVES 4–6

1 Combine the glutinous rice, brown sugar, half the coconut milk and all the water in a medium-sized saucepan.

2 Bring to the boil and simmer for about 15–20 minutes or until the rice has absorbed most of the liquid, stirring from time to time. Preheat the oven to 150°C/300°F/Gas 2.

3 Transfer all of the rice into one large ovenproof dish or divide it evenly between individual ramekins. Then mix together the eggs, remaining coconut milk and sugar in a bowl.

4 Strain the mixture and pour evenly over the par-cooked rice.

5 Place the dish in a baking tin. Pour in enough boiling water to come halfway up the sides of the dish.

6 Cover the dish with a piece of foil and bake in the oven for about 35 minutes to 1 hour or until the custard is set. Serve warm or cold, sprinkled with icing sugar.

MANGO ICE CREAM

Mangoes are used widely in Asian cooking, particularly in Thailand, where this deliciously rich ice cream originates.

INGREDIENTS
2 x 425g/15oz cans mango,
sliced and drained
50g/2oz/4 tbsp caster sugar
juice of 1 lime
15ml/1 tbsp powdered gelatine
350ml/12fl oz/1½ cups double cream,
lightly whipped
fresh mint sprigs, to decorate

SERVES 4–6

COOK'S TIP
Other fruits can be used in this recipe to make flavoursome ice creams. If you are looking for a dessert to serve after a spicy main course, choose sharp, tangy citrus fruits such as orange, lemon or grapefruit, which will cleanse and refresh the palate and aid digestion.

1 Reserve 4–6 slices of mango for decoration and chop the remainder into small cubes. Place in a bowl with the sugar. Add the lime juice to the mixture.

2 Put 45ml/3 tbsp hot water in a small bowl and sprinkle over the gelatine. Place over a pan of gently simmering water and stir until dissolved. Pour on to the cubed mango and mix well.

3 Add the lightly whipped cream and fold into the mango mixture. Pour the mixture into a polythene freezer bag or box and freeze until half frozen.

4 Place in a food processor or blender and blend until smooth. Spoon back into the polythene bag and refreeze.

5 Remove from the freezer 10 minutes before serving and place in the refrigerator. Serve scoops of the ice cream decorated with pieces of the reserved sliced mango, topped with sprigs of fresh mint.

STEWED PUMPKIN IN COCONUT CREAM

Stewed fruit is a popular dessert in Thailand. Use the firm-textured Japanese kabocha pumpkin for this dish, if you can. Bananas and melons can also be prepared in this way, or even sweet-corn kernels or pulses such as mung beans and black beans, in coconut milk.

INGREDIENTS
1kg/2¼lb kabocha pumpkin
750ml/1¼ pint/3 cups coconut milk
175g/6oz granulated sugar
pinch of salt
pumpkin seed kernels, toasted, and
mint sprigs, to decorate

SERVES 4–6

COOK'S TIP
Any pumpkin can be used for this dish, as long as it has a firm texture. Jamaican or New Zealand varieties both make good alternatives to kabocha pumpkin.

1 Wash the pumpkin skin and cut off most of it. Scoop out the seeds.

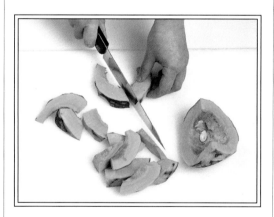

2 Using a sharp knife, cut the flesh into pieces about 5cm/2in in length and 2cm/¾in in thickness.

3 In a saucepan, bring the coconut milk, sugar and salt to the boil.

4 Add the pumpkin and simmer for about 10–15 minutes until the pumpkin is tender. Serve warm. Decorate each serving with a few toasted pumpkin seed kernels and a mint sprig.

COCONUT CUSTARD

This traditional dish from Thailand can be baked or steamed and is often served with a selection of fruit such as mangoes or tamarillos.

INGREDIENTS
4 eggs
75g/3oz/½ cup soft light brown sugar
250ml/8fl oz/1 cup coconut milk
5ml/1 tsp vanilla, rose or jasmine essence
mint leaves and icing sugar, to decorate
fruit slices, to serve

SERVES 4–6

1 Preheat the oven to 150°C/300°F/Gas 2. Whisk the eggs and sugar in a bowl until smooth. Add the coconut milk and the essence and blend well together.

2 Strain the mixture and pour into individual ramekins.

3 Stand the ramekins in a roasting pan. Carefully fill the roasting pan with hot water to reach halfway up the outside of the ramekins.

COOK'S TIP
To test whether custards are set, insert a fine skewer or cocktail stick into the centre of the ramekin. If it comes out clean, they are properly cooked and ready to remove from the oven.

4 Bake for about 35–40 minutes or until the custards are set. (See Cook's Tip.)

5 Remove from the oven and leave to cool. Turn out on to a plate, and serve with sliced fruit. Decorate with mint leaves and a sprinkling of icing sugar.

TAPIOCA PUDDING

This pudding, made from large, pearl tapioca and coconut milk and served warm, is much lighter than the western-style version. You can adjust the sweetness to your taste. Serve with lychees or the smaller, similar-tasting logans – also known as "dragon's eyes".

INGREDIENTS
115g/4oz tapioca
475ml/16fl oz/2 cups water
175g/6oz granulated sugar
pinch of salt
250ml/8fl oz/1 cup coconut milk
250g/9oz prepared tropical fruits
finely shredded rind of 1 lime,
to decorate

SERVES 4

1 Soak the tapioca in warm water for 1 hour so the grains swell. Drain.

2 Put the water in a saucepan and bring to the boil. Stir in the sugar and salt.

3 Add the tapioca and coconut milk and simmer for about 10 minutes.

4 Serve warm with tropical fruits and decorate with strips of lime rind.

MANGO WITH STICKY RICE

E veryone's favourite dessert. Mangoes, with their delicate fragrance, sweet and sour flavour and velvety flesh, blend especially well with coconut glutinous rice. You need to start preparing this dish the day before.

INGREDIENTS
115g/4oz white glutinous (sticky) rice
175ml/6fl oz/¾ cup thick
coconut milk
45ml/3 tbsp granulated sugar
pinch of salt
2 ripe mangoes
strips of lime rind, to decorate

SERVES 4

1 Rinse the glutinous rice thoroughly in several changes of cold water, until the water is clear, then leave to soak overnight in a bowl of fresh, cold water.

2 Drain the rice and spread in an even layer in a steamer lined with some cheesecloth. Cover and steam for about 20 minutes, or until the grains of rice are tender and succulent.

3 Meanwhile, reserve 45ml/3 tbsp of the top of the coconut milk and combine the rest with the sugar and salt in a saucepan. Bring to the boil, stirring until the sugar dissolves, then pour into a bowl and leave to cool a little.

4 Turn the rice into a bowl and pour over the coconut mixture. Stir, then leave for about 10–15 minutes.

5 Peel the mangoes and cut the flesh into slices. Place on top of the rice and drizzle over the reserved coconut milk. Decorate with strips of lime rind.

FRIED BANANAS

These delicious treats are a favourite among children and adults alike. They are sold as snacks throughout the day and night at portable roadside stalls in Thailand. Other fruits such as pineapples and apples work just as well.

INGREDIENTS
115g/4oz plain flour
2.5ml/½ tsp bicarbonate of soda
pinch of salt
30ml/2 tbsp granulated sugar
1 egg
90ml/6 tbsp water
30ml/2 tbsp shredded coconut,
or 15ml/1 tbsp sesame seeds
4 firm bananas
oil, for deep frying
lychees and sprigs of mint, to decorate
30ml/2 tbsp honey, to serve (optional)

SERVES 4

1 Sift the flour, bicarbonate of soda and salt into a bowl. Stir in the granulated sugar. Whisk in the egg and add enough water to make quite a thin batter.

2 Whisk in the shredded coconut or sesame seeds.

3 Peel the bananas. Carefully cut each one in half lengthways, and then crossways.

4 Heat the oil in a wok or deep frying pan. Dip the bananas in the batter, then deep-fry in batches in the oil until golden.

5 Remove from the oil and drain on kitchen paper. Decorate with lychees and sprigs of mint, and serve immediately with honey, if using.

TOFFEE APPLES, CHINESE-STYLE

A wide variety of other fruits, such as bananas and pineapples, can be cooked in this way. Sprinkle with sesame seeds for extra crunch.

INGREDIENTS
4 firm eating apples, peeled and cored
115g/4oz/1 cup plain flour
120ml/4fl oz/½ cup cold water
1 egg, beaten
vegetable oil, for deep-frying, plus 30ml/ 2 tbsp for the toffee
115g/4oz/½ cup sugar

SERVES 4

1 Cut each apple into 8 pieces. Dust each piece with a little of the flour.

2 Sift the remaining flour into a mixing bowl, then slowly add the cold water and stir to make a smooth batter. Add the beaten egg and blend well.

3 Heat the oil in a wok. Dip the apple pieces in the batter and deep-fry in batches for about 3 minutes or until golden *(left)*. Remove and drain. Heat 30ml/2 tbsp of the oil in the wok, add the sugar and stir constantly until the sugar has caramelized. Quickly add the apple pieces and blend well so that each piece of apple is coated with the "toffee". Dip the apple pieces into cold water to harden before serving.

LIME AND LYCHEE SALAD

This mixture of fruits in a tangy lime and lychee syrup, topped with a light sprinkling of toasted sesame seeds, makes a refreshing finish to a summer meal.

INGREDIENTS
115g/4oz/½ cup caster sugar
thinly pared rind and juice of 1 lime
400g/14oz can lychees in syrup
1 ripe mango, stoned and sliced
1 eating apple, cored and sliced
2 bananas, chopped
1 star fruit, sliced (optional)
5ml/1 tsp sesame seeds, toasted

SERVES 4

1 Place the sugar in a saucepan with 300ml/½ pint/1¼ cups water and the lime rind. Heat gently until the sugar dissolves, then increase the heat and boil gently for about 7–8 minutes. Remove from the heat and leave to cool.

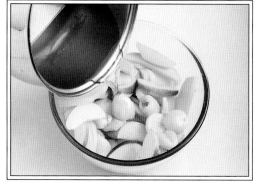

2 Drain the lychee juice into the lime syrup with the lime juice.

3 Place the lychees, mango, apple, bananas and star fruit, if using, in a large bowl and pour over the lime and lychee syrup *(left)*. Cover and chill for 1 hour. Remove from the fridge and ladle the fruit salad into a chilled serving bowl. Sprinkle with the toasted sesame seeds and serve.

PINEAPPLE BOATS

A variety of exotic fruits can be used for this fruit salad depending on what is available. Look out for mandarin oranges, star fruit, pawpaw, Cape gooseberries and passion fruit.

INGREDIENTS
75g/3oz/6 tbsp sugar
300ml/½ pint/1¼ cups water
30ml/2 tbsp stem ginger syrup
2 pieces star anise
2.5cm/1in piece cinnamon stick
1 clove
juice of ½ lemon
2 mint sprigs
1 mango
2 bananas, sliced
8 lychees, fresh or canned
*225g/8oz fresh strawberries, trimmed
and halved*
2 pieces stem ginger, cut into sticks
1 pineapple

SERVES 4–6

1 Put the sugar, water, ginger syrup, star anise, cinnamon, clove, lemon juice and mint into a saucepan. Bring to the boil and simmer for 3 minutes. Strain into a large bowl and allow to cool.

2 Slice off both the top and bottom from the mango and peel away the outer skin. Stand the mango on one end and remove the flesh in two pieces either side of the large flat stone. Slice the flesh evenly and add to the cooled syrup. Add the bananas, lychees, strawberries and ginger to the syrup. Cover and chill until ready to serve.

3 Cut the pineapple in half lengthways. Cut out the flesh to leave two boat shapes. Cut the flesh into large chunks and place in the cooled syrup.

4 Spoon the fruit into the pineapple halves and serve. There will be enough fruit left over to refill the pineapple halves.

231

AVOCADO AND LIME ICE CREAM

I n China, as in other parts of the world, avocados are frequently eaten as desserts. Their rich texture makes them perfect for a smooth, creamy and delicious ice cream.

INGREDIENTS
4 egg yolks
300ml/½ pint/1¼ cups whipping cream
115g/4oz/½ cup granulated sugar
2 ripe avocados
grated rind of 2 limes
juice of 1 lime
2 egg whites
fresh mint sprigs and avocado slices,
to decorate

SERVES 4–6

COOK'S TIP
Ice creams should be quite sweet before they are frozen since they lose some of their flavour when ice cold. Do not store ice cream for too long or ice crystals will form, which will spoil the texture.

1 Beat the egg yolks in a heatproof bowl. In a saucepan, heat the cream with the sugar, stirring it well until the sugar dissolves. As the cream rises to the top of the saucepan at the point of boiling, remove the pan from the heat.

2 Gently pour the beaten egg yolks into the scalded cream, adding them in small amounts from a height above the saucepan. This stops the mixture from curdling. Allow the mixture to cool, stirring occasionally, then chill.

3 Peel and mash the avocados until they are smooth then beat them into the chilled custard with the lime rind and juice. Check for sweetness.

4 Pour the mixture into a shallow container and freeze until slushy. Beat it well once or twice as it freezes to stop large ice crystals forming.

5 Whisk the egg whites until softly peaking and fold into mixture. Freeze until firm. Serve, decorated with mint and avocado.

RED BEAN PASTE PANCAKES

I f you can't find red bean paste, sweetened chestnut purée or mashed dates make good substitutes. Thin pancakes can be bought from Chinese supermarkets and frozen, or you can make your own.

INGREDIENTS
120ml/4floz/½ cup sweetened red bean paste
8 thin pancakes
30–45ml/2–3 tbsp vegetable oil
sugar, to serve

SERVES 4

COOK'S TIP
Cooked pancakes can be stored in the freezer. To reheat, warm in a steamer or in a microwave.

1 Spread about 15ml/1 tbsp of the red bean paste over about three-quarters of each pancake, then roll each pancake over three or four times.

2 Heat the oil in a wok or frying pan and shallow-fry the pancake rolls until golden brown, turning once.

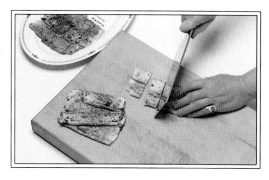

3 Cut each pancake roll into 3–4 pieces and sprinkle with sugar to serve.

THIN PANCAKES
To make 24–30 pancakes, sift 450g/1lb/4 cups plain flour into a bowl. Slowly stir in 300ml/½ pint/1¼ cups boiling water. Add 5ml/1tsp vegetable oil and mix to a firm dough. Cover with a damp cloth and leave to stand for 30 minutes. Lightly knead the dough on a floured surface for 5–8 minutes until smooth. Divide into three. Roll each piece into a cylinder, then cut into 8–10 pieces and roll into balls. Press flat, then roll into a 15cm/6in circle. Heat a small dry pan and cook one at a time until brown spots appear on the undersides. Stack the pancakes under a damp cloth until you have cooked all of them.

ALMOND CURD JUNKET

Also known as Almond Float, this dessert is usually thickened with agar-agar or isinglass, though gelatine can also be used. It comes from eastern China.

INGREDIENTS
*10g/¼oz agar-agar or isinglass or 25g/1oz
gelatine powder
600ml/1 pint/2½ cups water
50g/2oz/4 tbsp sugar
300ml/½ pint/1¼ cups milk
5ml/1 tsp almond essence
fresh or canned mixed fruit salad with
syrup, to serve*

SERVES 4–6

2 In a separate saucepan, dissolve the sugar in the remaining water over a medium heat. Add the milk and the almond essence, blending well, but do not boil.

3 Mix the milk and sugar with the agar-agar or isinglass mixture in a large serving bowl. When cool, place in the fridge for 2–3 hours to set.

1 In a saucepan, slowly dissolve the agar-agar or isinglass in half the water over a gentle heat. If using gelatine, follow the manufacturer's instructions.

4 To serve, cut the junket into small cubes and spoon into a serving dish or into individual bowls. Then pour the fruit salad, with the syrup, over the junket.

GREEN TEA CAKE

Baking cakes for desserts takes on a new twist when using Japanese ingredients. For example, glacé aduki beans *(ama-natto)* are used in the same way as marrons glacés, and the cake remains moist and light.

INGREDIENTS
115g/4oz/1 cup plain flour
15g/¹⁄₂oz green tea powder
2.5ml/¹⁄₂ tsp baking powder
3 size 3 eggs
75g/3oz/¹⁄₃ cup granulated sugar
75g/3oz/¹⁄₃ cup ama-natto (glacé Japanese aduki beans)
65g/2¹⁄₂oz/5 tbsp lightly salted butter, melted
whipped cream, to serve (optional)

*MAKES AN 18 X 7.5 X 10CM/
7 X 3 X 4IN CAKE*

1 *Preheat the oven to 180°C/350°F/Gas 4. Line and grease a loaf tin. Sift the flour, green tea powder and baking powder together and set aside.*

2 In a large heatproof bowl, whisk the eggs and sugar over a saucepan of hot water until pale and thick.

3 Sprinkle the sifted flour over the mixture. Before the flour sinks into the mixture, add the glacé Japanese aduki beans, then fold in the ingredients gently using a spatula. Fold the mixture over from the bottom once or twice. Do not mix too hard. Fold in the melted butter.

4 Pour the mixture into the prepared tin and smooth over the top. Bake the cake in the lower part of the oven for about 35–40 minutes, or until a warm metal skewer inserted into the centre of the cake comes out free of sticky mixture.

5 Turn out the cake on to a wire rack and remove the lining paper while it is hot. Leave to cool. Slice and serve with whipped cream, if liked.

RICE CAKES WITH STRAWBERRIES

W hereas traditionally an ingredient such as aduki bean paste would have been the sole accompaniment for these rice cakes, in this fairly modern dessert, fresh fruit is also served.

INGREDIENTS
100g/3¾ oz/scant ½ cup shiratama-ko powder (rice flour)
15ml/1 tbsp sugar
cornflour, for dusting
10 strawberries
115g/4oz/scant ½ cup canned neri-an *(Japanese soft aduki bean paste), cut into 5 pieces*

1 In a microwave-proof bowl, mix the shiratama-ko powder and sugar. Gradually add 200ml/7fl oz/scant 1 cup water. Knead well to make a thick paste.

2 Cover and cook in a microwave (600 or 500W) for 1½–2 minutes. Alternatively, steam it in a heatproof bowl over a pan of simmering water for 10–15 minutes.

3 Lightly dust a chopping board with a layer of cornflour. Turn out the heated mixture on to it and divide it into five even-size pieces. Using a rolling pin, gently roll out a portion of the mixture into a small oval shape.

4 Put a strawberry and a piece of *neri-an* in the middle. Fold the rice cake in half and serve decorated with a strawberry. Make a further four rice cakes. Eat the rice cakes on the day they are prepared – if left for any longer, they will harden.

SWEET POTATO, APPLE AND BEAN PASTE CAKES

A mixture of mashed sweet potato and a hint of apple is shaped into cubes, covered in batter and then seared in a hot pan to seal in the natural moisture. Aduki bean paste is also made into cakes by the same method.

INGREDIENTS
250g/9oz canned neri-an *(Japanese soft aduki bean paste), divided into 3 pieces*

FOR THE BATTER
90ml/6 tbsp plain flour
pinch of sugar
75ml/5 tbsp water

FOR THE STUFFING
150g/5oz sweet potato, peeled
¼ red eating apple, cored and peeled
200ml/7fl oz/scant 1 cup water
50g/2oz/¼ cup sugar
juice of ¼ lemon

SERVES 3 (MAKES 6)

1 Put all the ingredients for the batter in a bowl and mix well until smooth. Pour the batter into a large, shallow dish.

2 Dice the sweet potato and soak it in plenty of cold water for 5 minutes to remove any bitterness, then drain well.

3 Coarsely chop the apple and place in a saucepan. Add the water and sweet potato. Sprinkle in 7.5ml/1½ tsp sugar and cook over a moderate heat until the apple and potato are softened.

4 Add the lemon juice and remove the saucepan from the heat. Then drain the sweet potato and apple and crush them to a coarse paste in a mixing bowl with the remaining sugar.

5 Using your hands, shape the mixture into three cubes.

6 Heat a non-stick frying pan. Carefully coat a cube of stuffing mixture in batter, then, taking great care not to burn your fingers, sear each side of the cube on the hot frying pan until the batter has set and cooked through.

7 Repeat this procedure with the remaining stuffing mixture and with the *neri-an*, shaped into similar-size cubes. Arrange on small plates and serve hot or cold.

GREEN AND YELLOW LAYERED CAKES

This colourful two-tone dessert is made by squeezing contrasting mixtures in a small pouch of muslin or thin cotton. The Japanese title, *Chakin-shibori,* is derived from the preparation techniques in which *chakin* means a pouch shape and *shibori* means a moulding action.

INGREDIENTS
FOR THE YOLK MIXTURE (*KIMI-AN*)
6 large eggs
50g/2oz/¼ cup granulated sugar

FOR THE PEA MIXTURE (*ENDO-AN*)
200g/7oz/1¾ cups fresh peas, shelled
40g/11½oz/8 tsp sugar

MAKES 6

1 To make the yolk mixture, hard-boil the eggs. Remove the yolks and sieve them into a bowl. Press the yolk with a spatula, add the sugar and mix well.

2 To make the pea mixture, boil the peas for about 15 minutes, or until they are softened. Drain and place in a mortar, then crush the peas with a pestle and transfer them to a saucepan.

3 Add the sugar and cook, stirring continuously, until the paste is thick. Keep the mixture simmering but ensure that it does not scorch on the bottom of the pan.

4 Spread out the paste in a large dish to cool it down quickly. To maintain its green colour, it is important to cool the paste as quickly as possible.

5 Divide each of the mixtures into six portions. Wet a piece of muslin or thin cotton and wring it out well.

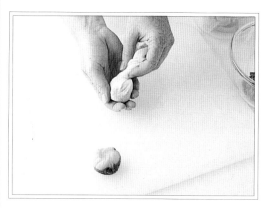

6 Place a lump of pea mixture on the cloth and put a lump of the yolk mixture on top. Wrap it up and squeeze the top of the cloth to mark a spiral pattern on the top of the cakes. Squeezing the cloth also joins the two stuffings together. Make another five cakes in the same way. Serve cold.

ACCOMPANIMENTS

In addition to well-spiced dishes, much of Asian cooking also features dipping sauces, pickles and other condiments on the table during a meal. Each cook puts a slightly different slant on a popular recipe, so feel free to adapt them to your taste. Hoisin Dip is basically a barbecue sauce and accompanies spring rolls and prawn crackers. Sambal Goreng and Thai Dipping Sauce are both strong and fiery. Indian breads are definitely worth learning to make if you have the time as the authentic flavours complement spicy dishes perfectly.

PARATHAS

Parathas are a richer, softer and flakier variation of chapatis, but they require a longer preparation time, so plan your menu well ahead.

INGREDIENTS
350g/12oz/3 cups atta *(wholemeal flour),*
plus extra for dusting
50g/2oz/½ cup plain flour
2.5ml/½ tsp salt
30ml/2 tbsp ghee
water, to mix
10ml/2 tsp ghee, melted

MAKES 12–15

1 Sift the flours and salt into a mixing bowl. Make a well in the centre and add the ghee. Rub in till the mixture resembles breadcrumbs. Slowly add enough water to make a soft but pliable dough. Cover and leave to rest for an hour.

2 Divide the dough into 12–15 portions and cover. Roll out each to a 10cm/4in round. Brush each round with a little of the melted ghee and dust with *atta*. Make a straight cut from the centre to the edge. Lift a cut edge and form the dough into a cone.

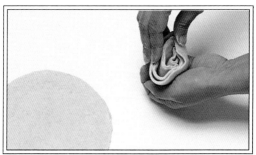

3 Flatten the cone into a ball, then roll out the dough to an 18cm/7in round. Heat a griddle and cook the parathas one at a time, brushing round the edges with the remaining ghee, until golden brown on each side. Serve hot.

NAAN BREAD

T raditionally, this flat leavened bread from northern India is baked in a tandoor or clay oven, though grilled naans look just as authentic.

INGREDIENTS
450g/1lb/4 cups plain flour
5ml/1 tsp baking powder
2.5ml/½ tsp salt
10ml/2 tsp sugar
10ml/2 tsp easy-blend dried yeast
210ml/7fl oz/scant 1 cup hand-hot milk
150ml/¼ pint/⅔ cup natural
yogurt, beaten
1 egg, beaten
60ml/4 tbsp melted ghee
flour, for dusting
chopped fresh coriander and onion seeds,
to sprinkle
ghee, for greasing
edible silver sheets, to serve (optional)

MAKES 6–8

1 Sift the flour, baking powder and salt into a large bowl. Stir in the sugar and easy-blend dried yeast. Make a well in the centre and add the milk, natural yogurt, egg and melted ghee. Gradually incorporate the flour mixture to make a pliable dough.

2 Knead the dough for about 10 minutes. Place in a bowl, cover tightly and keep in a warm place until the dough doubles in size. To test, push a finger into the dough – it should spring back. On a floured surface roll out the dough to a 5mm/¼in thickness.

3 Preheat the oven to 200°C/400°F/Gas 6. Roll out 6–8 slipper-shaped naans, about 25 × 15cm/10 × 6in tapering to about 5cm/2in. Sprinkle with the coriander and onion seeds. Bake on greased trays for 10–15 minutes. Serve hot, with silver, if using.

HOT
LIME PICKLE

A good lime pickle is delicious served with any meal. In India, where it originates, it is thought to increase the appetite and help digestion. It takes a long time to prepare, but is worth the wait!

INGREDIENTS
25 limes
225g/8oz/1 cup salt
50g/2oz/¼ cup fenugreek powder
50g/2oz/¼ cup mustard powder
150g/5oz/½ cup chilli powder
15g/½oz turmeric
600ml/1 pint/2½ cups mustard oil
5ml/1 tsp asafoetida
25g/1oz yellow mustard seeds, crushed

MAKES 450G/1LB/2 CUPS

1 Cut each lime into 8 pieces and remove the pips. Place the limes in a large sterilized jar or glass bowl. Add the salt and toss with the limes. Cover and leave in a warm place until they become soft and brown in colour, for about 1–2 weeks.

2 Mix together the fenugreek powder, mustard powder, chilli powder and turmeric and add to the limes. Cover with a clean cloth and leave to rest in a warm place for a further 2–3 days.

3 Heat the mustard oil in a frying pan and fry the asafoetida and mustard seeds. When the oil reaches smoking point, pour over the limes. Mix well, cover and leave in a warm place for 1 week before serving.

VIETNAMESE DIPPING SAUCE

Serve this dip in a small bowl as an accompaniment to spring rolls or meat dishes.

INGREDIENTS

1–2 small red chillies, seeded and finely chopped

1 garlic clove, crushed

10 g/¹/₄ oz/1 tbsp roasted peanuts

60 ml/4 tbsp coconut milk

30 ml/2 tbsp fish sauce

juice of 1 lime

10 ml/2 tsp sugar

15 ml/1 tbsp chopped coriander leaves

SERVES 4

MAKES 150ML/¹/₄ PINT/²/₃ CUP

1 Crush the red chilli together with the garlic and peanuts using a pestle and mortar or food processor. Transfer the mixture into a small bowl.

2 Add the coconut milk, fish sauce, lime juice, sugar and coriander and serve.

HOT TOMATO SAMBAL

Sambals are placed on the table as a condiment and are used mainly for dipping meat and fish. They are quite strong and should be used sparingly.

INGREDIENTS
3 ripe tomatoes
2.5ml/½ tsp salt
5ml/1 tsp chilli sauce
60ml/4 tbsp fish sauce or soy sauce
15ml/1 tbsp chopped coriander leaves

MAKES 120ML/4FL OZ/½ CUP

COOK'S TIP
Hot Tomato Sambal is often used in place of fresh red chillies in many sauces or curries. It can be stored in the refrigerator for up to a week.

1 Cover the tomatoes with boiling water to loosen the skins. Remove the skins, halve, discard the seeds and chop finely.

2 Place the tomatoes in a bowl, add the salt, chilli sauce and fish sauce or soy sauce. Sprinkle with coriander and serve.

SAMBAL GORENG

his sambal makes an excellent, if fiery, side dip for vegetable, fish or meat dishes.

INGREDIENTS
2.5cm/1in cube terasi
2 onions, quartered
2 garlic cloves, crushed
2.5cm/1in lengkuas, *peeled and sliced*
10ml/2 tsp chilli sambal paste or 2 fresh
red chillies, seeded and sliced
30ml/2 tbsp oil
45ml/3 tbsp tomato purée
600ml/1 pint/2½ cups stock or water
350g/12oz cooked chicken pieces
50g/2oz/⅓ cup cooked French beans
60ml/4 tbsp tamarind juice
pinch of sugar
45ml/3 tbsp coconut milk or cream
salt and freshly ground black pepper

MAKES 900ML/1 ½ PINTS/3¾ CUPS

COOK'S TIP
For Prawn Sambal Goreng, add 350g/12oz cooked prawns and 1 green pepper, seeded and chopped. For an egg version, add 3 hard-boiled eggs, shelled and chopped, and 2 tomatoes, skinned, seeded and chopped

1 Process the *terasi* with the onions and garlic to a paste in a food processor or with a pestle and mortar. Add the *lengkuas*, chilli sambal paste or sliced chillies and salt. Process or pound to a fine paste.

2 Fry the paste in hot oil for 1–2 minutes, without browning, until the mixture gives off a rich aroma.

3 Add the tomato purée and the stock or water and cook over a medium heat for 10 minutes. Add the chicken and French beans (or see Cook's Tip for alternatives) and cook for 3–4 minutes. Stir in the tamarind juice, sugar and coconut milk or cream at the last minute. Season with salt and freshly ground black pepper and serve immediately in small dipping bowls.

THAI DIPPING SAUCE

am Prik is the most common dipping sauce in Thailand. It has a fiery strength, so use with caution.

INGREDIENTS
15ml/1 tbsp vegetable oil
1 piece shrimp paste, 1cm/½ in square, or
15ml/1 tbsp fish sauce
2 cloves garlic, finely sliced
1 piece fresh ginger, 2cm/¾ in long, peeled
and finely chopped
3 small red chillies, seeded and chopped
15ml/1 tbsp finely chopped
coriander root or stem
20ml/4 tsp sugar
45ml/3 tbsp dark soy sauce
juice of ½ lime

MAKES 120ML/4FL OZ/½ CUP

COOK'S TIP
Nam Prik sauce will keep in a screw-top jar for up to 10 days or up to 2 weeks if stored in the refrigerator. As it is such a versatile sauce, suited to many Asian dishes, it's a good idea to make a large quantity as it can be frozen for up to 2 months.

1 Heat the vegetable oil in a wok, add the shrimp paste or fish sauce, garlic, ginger and chillies and soften without colouring, for about 1–2 minutes.

2 Remove from the heat and add the coriander, sugar, soy sauce and lime juice. Serve in a small bowl.

HOISIN DIP

This speedy dip needs no cooking and can be made in just a few minutes – it tastes great with spring rolls or prawn crackers.

INGREDIENTS
4 spring onions
4cm/1½in piece root ginger
2 red chillies
2 garlic cloves
60ml/4 tbsp hoisin sauce
120ml/4fl oz/½ cup passata
5ml/1 tsp sesame oil (optional)

SERVES 4

COOK'S TIP
Hoisin sauce makes an excellent base for full-flavour dips, especially when combining crunchy vegetables and other Oriental seasonings.

1 Trim off and discard the green ends of the spring onions. Slice the remainder very thinly. Peel the ginger with a swivel-bladed vegetable peeler, then chop it finely.

2 Halve the chillies lengthways and remove their seeds. Finely slice the flesh widthways into tiny strips. Finely chop the garlic. Stir together the hoisin sauce, passata, spring onions, ginger, chilli, garlic and sesame oil, if using, and serve within 1 hour.

INDEX

aduki beans, 7
  Green Tea Cake, 237
  Rice Cakes with Strawberries, 238
  Sweet Potato, Apple and Bean Paste
    Cakes, 239
agar-agar: Almond Curd Junket, 236
almonds, 7
  Almond Curd Junket, 236
  Chicken and Almond Soup, 18
  Spiced Okra with Almonds, 150
ama-natto: Green Tea Cake, 237
apples:
  Fruit and Raw Vegetable
    Gado-gado, 164
  Lime and Lychee Salad, 230
  Sweet Potato, Apple and Bean Paste
    Cakes, 239
  Toffee Apples, Chinese-style, 229
asparagus:
  Deep Fried Tofu and Asparagus in
    Stock, 178
  Fried Swordfish, 81
  Stir-fried Scallops with Asparagus, 63
aubergines, 7
  Balti Lamb-stuffed Vegetables, 120
  Green Beef Curry with Thai
    Aubergine, 128
  Spiced Aubergines, 152
avocados: Avocado and Lime Ice
  Cream, 232

Baked Fish in Banana Leaves, 58
Baked Rice Pudding, Thai-style, 219
Balinese Spiced Duck, 105
Balti Fish in Coconut Sauce, 54
Balti Lamb-stuffed Vegetables, 120
Balti Poussins in Tamarind Sauce, 90
bamboo shoots, 7
Bamboo Shoot Salad, 159
Balti Chicken with Lentils, 89
banana leaves: 7
  Baked Fish in Banana Leaves, 58
  Steamed Seafood Packets, 26

bananas:
  Fried Bananas, 228
  Lime and Lychee Salad, 230
  Pineapple Boats, 231
  Barbecued Chicken, 95
basil, 7
  Stir-fried Chicken with Basil and
    Chillies, 96
Basmati rice, 7
bay leaves, 7
bean curd: Spinach and Bean Curd
  Soup, 23
bean sauce, 7
beancurd, 7
beansprouts, 7
  Five-flavour Noodles, 206
  Noodles with Vegetables, 202
  Special Chow Mein, 200
  Sweet and Sour Noodles, 203
  Tofu Stir-fry, 161
beef:
  Beef and Vegetables on a Hot
    Plate, 142
  Dry-fried Shredded Beef, 136
  Fragrant Thai Meatballs, 126
  Green Beef Curry with Thai
    Aubergine, 128
  Hanoi Beef and Noodle Soup, 30
  Mussaman Curry, 124
  Rendang, 132
  Steak Bowl, 141
  Stir-fried Beef with Orange and
    Ginger, 134
  Stir-fried Beef in Oyster Sauce, 127
  Thai Beef Salad, 130
  Vegetable-stuffed Beef Rolls, 144
biryani: Chicken Biryani, 92
Boiled Fried Tofu with Hijiki Seaweed, 176
bok choy, 7
bonito, 7
  Spinach with Bonito Flakes, 44
Braised Fish with Mushrooms, 70
Braised Vegetables, 172
  Chicken with Chinese Vegetables, 110

Mu Shu Pork with Eggs and
  Mushrooms, 138
Red Chicken Curry with Bamboo
  Shoots, 98
Steamed Seafood Packets, 26
broccoli:
  Noodles with Vegetables, 202
  Stir-fried Mixed Vegetables, 163
Brussels sprouts: Stir-fried Brussels
  Sprouts, 168

cabbage:
  Braised Vegetables, 172
  Cabbage Salad, 162
  Deep Fried Pork Strips with
    Shredded Cabbage, 146
  Five-flavour Noodles, 206
  Karahi Shredded Cabbage with
    Cumin, 156
  Noodles with Vegetables, 202
  Spicy Cabbage, 155
  Stir-fried Mixed Vegetables, 163
  Tofu Stir-fry, 161
cakes:
  Green Tea Cake, 237
  Green and Yellow Layered Cakes, 240
  Rice Cakes with Strawberries, 238
cardamom pods 7
  Saffron and Cardamom Rice, 186
carrots:
  Chicken and Vegetable Stir-fry, 109
  Mixed Vegetable Soup, 174
  Stir-fried Mixed Vegetables, 163
  Stir-fried Pork with Vegetables, 137
  Tofu and Crunchy Vegetables, 170

cashew nuts, 7
  Chicken in a Cashew Nut Sauce, 94
Cauliflower with Coconut, 157
chana dhal, 7
  Lentils with Lamb and Tomatoes, 122
chapati flour, 7
chayote: Tamarind and Vegetable
  Soup, 34
Chiang Mai Noodle Soup, 192
Chiang Mai Salad, 102
chick-peas, 7
chicken:
  Barbecued Chicken, 95
  Balti Chicken with Lentils, 88
  Chiang Mai Noodle Soup, 192
  Chiang Mai Salad, 102
  Chicken and Almond Soup, 18
  Chicken Biryani, 92
  Chicken Cakes with Teriyaki Sauce, 49
  Chicken in a Cashew Nut Sauce, 94
  Chicken with Chinese Vegetables, 110
  Chicken Pasanda, 87
  Chicken and Vegetable Stir-fry, 109
  Chilli Chicken, 86
  Egg Fried Noodles, 196
  Hot and Sour Chicken Salad, 104
  Individual Noodle Casseroles, 208
  Indonesian Pork and Prawn Rice, 194
  Khara Masala Chicken, 84
  Kung Po Chicken, Szechuan Style, 112
  Mixed Rice, 204
  Red Chicken Curry with Bamboo
    Shoots, 98
  Sambal Goreng, 249
  Soy-braised Chicken, 113
  Special Chow Mein, 200
  Spicy Chicken and Mushroom Soup, 19
  Stir-fried Chicken with Basil and
    Chillies, 96
  Sweet and Sour Noodles, 203
  Tangy Chicken Salad, 100
  Thai Chicken Soup, 24
  Yakitori Chicken, 48
Chilled Noodles, 205

Chilli Crabs, 65
chilli powder, 8
chillies, 8
    Chilli Chicken, 86
    Chilli Crabs, 65
    chopping, 14
    Stir-fried Chicken with Basil and
        Chillies, 96
chow mein:
    Seafood Chow Mein, 198
    Special Chow Mein, 200
cinnamon, 8
cloves, 8
coconut, 8
    Balti Fish in Coconuut Sauce, 56
    Cauliflower with Coconut, 157
    Kashmir Coconut Fish, 56
coconut milk, 8
    Coconut Custard, 224
    Coconut Rice, 188
    Curried Prawns in Coconut Milk, 59
    Mixed Vegetables in Coconut Milk, 158
    Stewed Pumpkin in Coconut
        Cream, 222
    Colourful Pullao Rice, 184
coriander seeds, 8
courgettes: Tofu and Crunchy
    Vegetables, 170
crab:
Chilli Crabs, 65
    Golden Pouches, 25
    Steamed Seafood Packets, 26
    Vietnamese Spring Rolls, 32
cream: Mango Ice Cream, 220
Crispy Aromatic Duck, 106
Crispy Seaweed, 169
cucumber:
    Fish Cakes with Cucumber Relish, 29
    Fruit and Raw Vegetable
        Gado-gado, 164
    Simple Rolled Sushi, 46
cumin, 8
    Karahi Shredded Cabbage with.
    Cumin, 156

curries:
    Curried Prawns in Coconut Milk, 59
    Green Beef Curry with Thai
        Aubergine, 128
    Malaysian Fish Curry, 64
    Mussaman Curry, 124
    Red Chicken Curry with Bamboo
        Shoots, 98
    Tofu and Green Bean Red Curry, 160
curry leaves, 8
curry paste, 8

dashi, 8
Deep Fried Pork Strips with Shredded
    Cabbage, 146
Deep Fried Tofu and Asparagus
    in Stock, 178
dip: Hoisin Dip, 250
dried mushrooms, 8
Dry-fried Shredded Beef, 136
duck:
    Balinese Spiced Duck, 105
    Crispy Aromatic Duck, 106

egg noodles, 8
    Chiang Mai Noodle Soup, 192
    Egg Fried Noodles, 196
    Five-flavour Noodles, 206
    Fruit and Raw Vegetable
        Gado-gado, 164
    Noodles with Chicken, Prawns and
        Ham, 202
    Noodles with Vegetables, 202
    Seafood Chow Mein, 198
    Soft Fried Noodles, 197

Special Chow Mein, 200
Sweet and Sour Noodles, 203
Thai Chicken Soup, 26
Tofu and Crunchy Vegetables, 170
see also noodles
eggs:
    Baked Rice Pudding, Thai-style, 219
    Coconut Custard, 224
    Egg Fried Noodles, 196
    Fruit and Raw Vegetable Gado-gado, 164
    Green and Yellow Layered Cakes, 240
    Kulfi, 212
    Mango Sorbet with Mango Sauce, 216
    Mu Shu Pork with Eggs and
        Mushrooms, 138
    Prawn and Egg-knot Soup, 40
    Prawn Fu-yung, 68
    Salmon sealed with Egg, 80
    Shiitake Mushroom and Egg Soup, 40
evaporated milk: Kulfi, 212

fennel seeds, 8
fenugreek, 8
fish:
    Baked Fish in Banana Leaves, 58
    Balti Fish in Coconut Sauce, 54
    Braised Fish with Mushrooms, 70
    Fish Cakes with Cucumber Relish, 29
    Five-spice Fish, 71
    Grilled Fish Masala, 52
    Kashmir Coconut Fish, 56
    Malaysian Fish Curry, 64
    Steamed Fish with Ginger, 72
fish sauce, 8
Five-flavour Noodles, 206
Five-spice Fish, 71
five-spice powder, 8
Fragrant Thai Meatballs, 126
French beans:
    Chicken and Vegetable Stir-fry, 109
    French beans with Sesame Seeds, 173
    Sambal Goreng, 249
    Tamarind and Vegetable Soup, 34
    Tofu Stir-fry, 161

Fried Bananas, 228
Fried Swordfish, 81
Fruit and Raw Vegetable Gado-gado, 164
fruit salad: Almond Curd Junket, 236
Fruity Pullao, 184

galangal, 8
garam masala, 9
    Home-made Garam Masala, 12
gari: Simple Rolled Sushi, 46
garlic, 9
Garlic Mushrooms, 35
ginger, 9
    Ginger Pork with Black Bean
        Sauce, 140
    Steamed Fish with Ginger, 72
    Stir-fried Beef with Orange and
        Ginger, 134
Golden Pouches, 25
green beans:
    Fish Cakes with Cucumber Relish, 29
    Special Chow Mein, 200
    Tofu and Green Bean Red Curry, 160
Green Beef Curry with Thai
    Aubergine, 128
    Green Tea Cake, 237
    Grilled Fish Masala, 52
    Grilled Prawns, 20

haddock: Kashmir Coconut Fish, 56
Hanoi Beef and Noodle Soup, 30
hoisin sauce, 9
    Hoisin Dip, 251
Home-made Garam Masala, 12
Hot Lime Pickle, 246
Hot and Sour Chicken Salad, 104
Hot and Sour Prawn Soup with Lemon
    Grass, 24
Hot Tomato Sambal, 248

ice cream:
    Avocado and Lime Ice Cream, 232
    Mango Ice Cream, 220
Individual Noodle Casseroles, 208

Indonesian Pork and Prawn Rice, 194
isinglass: Almond Curd Junket, 236

julienne strips, cutting, 15

kaffir lime, 9
Karahi Shredded Cabbage with
    Cumin, 156
Kashmir Coconut Fish, 56
Khara Masala Chicken, 84
Khara Masala Lamb, 118
kombu, 9
    Mooli with Sesame Miso Sauce, 45
konnyaku, 9
Mixed Vegetable Soup, 174
Kulfi, 212
Kung Po Chicken, Szechuan Style, 112

lamb:
    Balti Lamb-stuffed Vegetables, 120
    Khara Masala Lamb, 118
    Lamb with Spinach, 116
    Lentils with Lamb and Tomatoes, 122
lap cheong: Special Chow Mein, 200
lapsang souchong tea: Marbled Quail's
    Eggs, 38
Lassi, 215
leeks:
    Tofu and Crunchy Vegetables, 170
    Winter Tofu and Vegetables, 177
lemon grass, 9
    Hot and Sour Prawn Soup with Lemon
        Grass, 242
    Pan-steamed Mussels with Thai
        Herbs, 28
    peeling and chopping, 14
lemon sole: Braised Fish with
    Mushrooms, 70
lengkuas, 9
    Rendang, 132
    Sambal Goreng, 249
    Tamarind and Vegetable Soup, 34
Lentils with Lamb and Tomatoes, 122
lettuce: Beef and Vegetables on a Hot

Plate, 142
Lime and Lychee Salad, 230
limes:
    Avocado and Lime Ice Cream, 232
    Hot Lime Pickle, 246
    Lime and Lychee Salad, 230
lychees:
    Lime and Lychee Salad, 230
    Pineapple Boats, 231

mackerel: poached Mackerel with
    Miso, 80
Malaysian Fish Curry, 64
mange-touts:
    Braised Vegetables, 172
    Chicken with Chinese Vegetables, 110
    Mixed Rice, 204
    Red and White Prawns, 73
    Salmon sealed with Egg, 78
    Seafood Chow Mein, 198
    Stir-fried Pork with Vegetables, 137
    Stir-fried Turkey with Mange-touts, 108
    Sweet and Sour Noodles, 203
mangoes:
    Lime and Lychee Salad, 230
    Mango Ice Cream, 220
    Mango Sorbet with Mango Sauce, 216
    Mango with Sticky Rice, 227
Marbled Quail's Eggs, 36
meat: chopping meat for stir-frying, 15
meatballs: Fragrant Thai Meatballs, 126
mirin, 9
miso, 9
    Miso Soup, 41
    Mooli with Sesame Miso Sauce, 45
    poached Mackerel with Miso, 82
Mixed Rice, 204
Mixed Vegetables in Coconut Milk, 158
mooli, 9
    Beef and Vegetables on a Hot
        Plate, 142
    Mixed Vegetable Soup, 174
    Mooli with Sesame Miso Sauce, 45
    Prawn Tempura, 42

Sliced Raw Salmon, 75
Mu Shu Pork with Eggs and
    Mushrooms, 138
mushrooms:
    Braised Fish with Mushrooms, 70
    Braised Vegetables, 172
    Garlic Mushrooms, 35
    Golden Pouches, 25
    Hot and Sour Prawn Soup with Lemon
        Grass, 22
    Individual Noodle Casseroles, 208

Mixed Rice, 204
Mixed Vegetable Soup, 174
Mu Shu Pork with Eggs and
    Mushrooms, 138
Noodles with Vegetables, 202
Pak Choi and Mushroom Stir-fry, 166
Shiitake Mushroom and Egg Soup, 40
Spicy Chicken and Mushroom Soup, 19
Stir-fried Beef in Oyster Sauce, 127
Stir-fried Pork with Vegetables, 137
Tofu and Crunchy Vegetables, 170
Tofu and Green Bean Red Curry, 160
Vietnamese Spring Rolls, 32
Winter Tofu and Vegetables, 177
see also shiitake mushrooms
Mussaman Curry, 124
mussels: Pan-steamed Mussels with Thai
    Herbs, 28
mustard seeds, 9

Naan Bread, 245
neri-an:
    Rice Cakes with Strawberries, 238

Sweet Potato, Apple and Bean Paste
    Cakes, 239
noodles, 10
    Chilled Noodles, 205
    Hanoi Beef and Noodle Soup, 30
    Individual Noodle Casseroles, 208
    Noodles with Chicken, Prawns and
        Ham, 202
    Noodles with Vegetables, 202
    Vietnamese Spring Rolls, 32
    see also egg noodles
nori, 10
nuts: Quick Basmati and Nut Pilaff, 182

octopus: Shaped Sushi, 78
okra: Spiced Okra with Almonds, 150
onion seeds, 10
oranges:
    Oranges with Saffron Yogurt, 214
    Stir-fried Beef with Orange and
        Ginger, 134
oyster sauce, 10
    Stir-fried Beef in Oyster Sauce, 127

palm sugar, 10
Pan-steamed Mussels with Thai Herbs, 28
pancakes:
    Crispy Aromatic Duck, 106
    Red Bean Paste Pancakes, 234
Parathas, 244
pears: Fruit and Raw Vegetable
    Gado-gado, 164
peas: Green and Yellow Layered
    Cakes, 240
peppercorns, 10
peppers:
    Balti Lamb-stuffed Vegetables, 120
    Chicken and Vegetable Stir-fry, 109
    Five-flavour Noodles, 206
pickles, 10
    Hot Lime Pickle, 246
pilaff: Quick Basmati and Nut Pilaff, 182
pineapples:
    Fruit and Raw Vegetable

Gado-gado, 164
Pineapple Boats, 231
Pineapple Fried Rice, 189
pistachios: Kulfi, 212
plaice: Braised Fish with Mushrooms, 70
Poached Mackerel with Miso, 80
pak choi:
    Noodles with Vegetables, 202
    Pak Choi and Mushroom Stir-fry, 166
pomegranate seeds, 10
    Prawns with Pomegranate Seeds, 20
ponzu dip, 142
pork:
    Deep Fried Pork Strips with Shredded
        Cabbage, 146
    Fragrant Thai Meatballs, 126
    Ginger Pork with Black Bean
        Sauce, 140
    Golden Pouches, 27
    Indonesian Pork and Prawn Rice, 194
    Mu Shu Pork with Eggs and
        Mushrooms, 138
    Pineapple Fried Rice, 189
    Pork Satay, 33
    Stir-fried Pork with Vegetables, 137
    Sweet and Sour Pork, Thai-style, 131
potatoes:
    Chicken Biryani, 92
    Mussaman Curry, 124
    Rendang, 132
    Spiced Spinach and Potatoes, 154
poussins: Balti Poussins in Tamarind
    Sauce, 90
prawns:
    Beef and Vegetables on a Hot
        Plate, 142
    Curried Prawns in Coconut Milk, 59
    Grilled Prawns, 20
    Hot and Sour Prawn Soup with Lemon
        Grass, 22
    Indonesian Pork and Prawn Rice, 194

    Pineapple Fried Rice, 189
    Prawn and Egg-knot Soup, 38

Prawn Fu-yung, 68
Prawn Tempura, 42
Prawns with Pomegranate Seeds, 20
Red and White Prawns, 73
Satay Prawns, 60
Seafood Chow Mein, 198
Shaped Sushi, 76
Special Chow Mein, 200
Steamed Seafood Packets, 26
Stir-fried Seafood, 66

Thai Fried Noodles, 190
Thai Prawn Salad, 62
Vietnamese Spring Rolls, 32
pullao: Fruity Pullao, 184
pumpkin: Stewed Pumpkin in Coconut
    Cream, 222

quail's eggs:
    Fruit and Raw Vegetable
        Gado-gado, 164
    Marbled Quail's Eggs, 36
Quick Basmati and Nut Pilaff, 182

radish: Thai Fried Noodles, 190
red bean paste, 10
    Red Bean Paste Pancakes, 234
Red Chicken Curry with Bamboo
    Shoots, 98
red mullet: Steamed Fish with Ginger, 72
Red and White Prawns, 73
relish, cucumber, 29
Rendang, 132
rice:
    Baked Rice Pudding, Thai-style, 219

Bamboo Shoot Salad, 159
Chicken Biryani, 92
Coconut Rice, 188
Indonesian Pork and Prawn Rice, 194
Mango with Sticky Rice, 227
Mixed Rice, 204
Mooli with Sesame Miso Sauce, 47
Pineapple Fried Rice, 189
Quick Basmati and Nut Pilaff, 182
Saffron and Cardamom Rice, 186
Shaped Sushi, 76
Simple Rolled Sushi, 46
Steak Bowl, 141
Tomato Rice, 187
rice noodles: Thai Fried Noodles, 190
rice sheets:
    Steamed Seafood Packets, 26
    Vietnamese Spring Rolls, 32
rice vinegar, 10
rice wine, 10

saffron, 10
Oranges with Saffron Yogurt, 214
Saffron and Cardamom Rice, 186
sake, 10
salads:
Bamboo Shoot Salad, 159
Cabbage Salad, 162
Chiang Mai Salad, 102
Hot and Sour Chicken Salad, 104
Lime and Lychee Salad, 230
Tangy Chicken Salad, 100
Thai Beef Salad, 130
Thai Prawn Salad, 62
salmon:
Salmon sealed with Egg, 78
Shaped Sushi, 76
Simple Rolled Sushi, 46
Sliced Raw Salmon, 75
sambals:
    Hot Tomato Sambal, 250
    Sambal Goreng, 249
Satay Prawns, 60
sauces:

black bean, 140
cashew nut, 94
coconut, 54
gomaae, 173
mango, 216
peanut, 60, 126, 164
satay, 33
sesame miso, 45
tamarind, 90
teriyaki, 49, 81
Thai Dipping, 250
tonkatsu, 146
yakitori, 48
scallops:
    Seafood Chow Mein, 198
    Stir-fried Scallops with Asparagus, 63
    Stir-fried Seafood, 66
sea bass: Steamed Fish with Ginger, 72
Seafood Chow Mein, 198
seaweed:
    Boiled Fried Tofu with Hijiki
        Seaweed, 176
    Chilled Noodles, 205
    Crispy Seaweed, 169
    Five-flavour Noodles, 206
    Miso Soup, 41
    Simple Rolled Sushi, 46
    Tuna Rice Bowl, 74
    Winter Tofu and Vegetables, 177
sesame oil, 10
sesame seeds, 10
French beans with Sesame Seeds, 173
Mooli with Sesame Miso Sauce, 45
seven-flavour spice or pepper, 11
shallots, 11
Shaped Sushi, 76
shiitake mushrooms, 11
    Beef and Vegetables on a Hot
        Plate, 142
    Chicken with Chinese Vegetables, 110
    Pok Choi and Mushroom Stir-fry, 166
    Shiitake Mushroom and Egg Soup, 40
    see also mushrooms
shiratama-ko powder, 11

Rice Cakes with Strawberries, 240
shiso leaves, 11
shrimps:
    Spinach and Bean Curd Soup, 23
    Thai Fried Noodles, 190
Simple Rolled Sushi, 46
Sliced Raw Salmon, 75
Soft Fried Noodles, 197
sorbets: Mango Sorbet with Mango
    Sauce, 216
soups:
    Chiang Mai Noodle Soup, 192
    Chicken and Almond Soup, 18
    Hanoi Beef and Noodle Soup, 30
    Hot and Sour Prawn Soup with Lemon
        Grass, 22
    Miso Soup, 41
    Mixed Vegetable Soup, 174
    Prawn and Egg-knot Soup, 38
    Shiitake Mushroom and Egg Soup, 40
    Spicy Chicken and Mushroom Soup, 19
    Spinach and Bean Curd Soup, 23
    Tamarind and Vegetable Soup, 34
    Thai Chicken Soup, 24
soy sauce, 11
Soy-braised Chicken, 113
Special Chow Mein, 200
Spiced Aubergines, 152
Spiced Okra with Almonds, 150
Spiced Spinach and Potatoes, 154
Spicy Cabbage, 155
Spicy Chicken and Mushroom Soup, 19
spinach:
    Individual Noodle Casseroles, 208
    Lamb with Spinach, 116
    Spiced Spinach and Potatoes, 154
    Spinach and Bean Curd Soup, 23
    Spinach with Bonito Flakes, 44
spring greens: Crispy Seaweed, 169
spring rolls: Vietnamese Spring Rolls, 32
squid:
    Egg Fried Noodles, 196
    Seafood Chow Mein, 198
    Shaped Sushi, 76

Stir-fried Seafood, 66
star anise, 11
star fruit: Lime and Lychee Salad, 230
Steak Bowl, 141
Steamed Fish with Ginger, 72
Steamed Seafood Packets, 26
Stewed Pumpkin in Coconut Cream, 222
Stir-fried Beef with Orange and
    Ginger, 134
Stir-fried Beef in Oyster Sauce, 127
Stir-fried Brussels Sprouts, 168
Stir-fried Chicken with Basil and
    Chillies, 96
Stir-fried Mixed Vegetables, 163
Stir-fried Pork with Vegetables, 137
Stir-fried Scallops with Asparagus, 63
Stir-fried Seafood, 66
Stir-fried Turkey with Mange-touts, 108
strawberries:
    Pineapple Boats, 231
    Rice Cakes with Strawberries, 238
sultanas: Fruity Pullao, 184
sushi, 11
    Shaped Sushi, 76
    Simple Rolled Sushi, 46
    sushi vinegar, 11
    sushimi, 10
Sweet Potato, Apple and Bean Paste
    Cakes, 239
Sweet and Sour Noodles, 203
Sweet and Sour Pork, Thai-style, 131
sweetcorn:
    Garlic Mushrooms, 35
    Noodles with Vegetables, 202
    Stir-fried Mixed Vegetables, 163
    Sweet and Sour Noodles, 203
    Tamarind and Vegetable Soup, 34
    Tofu and Crunchy Vegetables, 170
    Tofu Stir-fry, 161
swordfish: Fried Swordfish, 79
Szechuan peppercorns, 11, 36

tamarind, 11
    Balti Poussins in Tamarind Sauce, 90

Tamarind and Vegetable Soup, 34
Tangy Chicken Salad, 100
Tapioca Pudding, 226
tea:
Green Tea Cake, 237
Marbled Quail's Eggs, 36
tempura: Prawn Tempura, 42
terasi, 11
Indonesian Pork and Prawn Rice, 194
Sambal Goreng, 249

Tamarind and Vegetable Soup, 34
teriyaki:
    Chicken Cakes with Teriyaki Sauce, 49
    Teriyaki Trout, 81
Thai Beef Salad, 130
Thai Chicken Soup, 24
Thai Dipping Sauce, 250
Thai Fried Noodles, 190
Thai Prawn Salad, 62
Thai Red Curry Paste, 13
Toffee Apples, Chinese-style, 229
tofu, 11
    Boiled Fried Tofu with Hijiki
        Seaweed, 176
    Braised Vegetables, 172
    Deep Fried Tofu and Asparagus in
        Stock, 178
    Garlic Mushrooms, 35
    Miso Soup, 41
    Mixed Rice, 204
    Mixed Vegetable Soup, 174
    Tofu and Crunchy Vegetables, 170
    Tofu and Green Bean Red Curry, 160
    Tofu Stir-fry, 161

Winter Tofu and Vegetables, 177
tomatoes:
    Fruit and Raw Vegetable
        Gado-gado, 164
    Hot Tomato Sambal, 248
    Lentils with Lamb and Tomatoes, 122
    Tomato Rice, 187
trout:
    Steamed Fish with Ginger, 72
    Teriyaki Trout, 81
tuna:
    Shaped Sushi, 76
    Simple Rolled Sushi, 46
    Tuna Rice Bowl, 74
turkey: Stir-fried Turkey with
    Mange-touts, 108
turmeric, 11

Vegetable-stuffed Beef Rolls, 144
Vermicelli Pudding, 218
Vietnamese Dipping Sauce, 247
Vietnamese Spring Rolls, 32
vinegar, 11

wakame seaweed, 11
    Miso Soup, 41
wasabi, 11
water chestnuts:
    Steamed Seafood Packets, 26
    Stir-fried Turkey with Mange-touts, 108
    Winter Tofu and Vegetables, 177
wonton wrappers, 11
    Golden Pouches, 25

Yakitori Chicken, 48
yellow bean paste, 11
yogurt:
    Lassi, 217
    Oranges with Saffron Yogurt, 214